What If

To Keazzi
with all my love
x x

What If

**Does our consciousness survive
our physical existence?**

Are we both Physical
and Spiritual?

**A profound and fascinating book written with
humour, love and warmth. This transformational
work, is a must read, for those trying to understand
the process of what it is to be a human.**

**This never to be forgotten read, will
enable a paradigm shift in your
Expectations for this life and beyond**

Michael Brookes

To order additional copies of this book, contact:
Xlibris
UK TFN: 0800 0148620 (Toll Free inside the UK)
UK Local: (02) 0369 56328 (+44 20 3695 6328 from outside the UK)
www.Xlibrispublishing.co.uk
Orders@Xlibrispublishing.co.uk
847998

Dedication

I dedicate this modest little book to "Universal Consciousness" for its consistent, unsought, yet amazingly transformational, and beneficial involvement throughout my life.

I also make this dedication to three women. The first, you will hear about later. Although there were many motivations and reasons to write this book, the first, and most compelling, was my wife, now deceased. The other woman I make this dedication to, is my youngest daughter Naomi, who despite having to have me for her Dad, functions as the glue that holds the rest of the family together.

Finally, but by no means least, is Keazzi, the beautiful and deeply spiritual person who, despite I'm sure, her much better judgment, accepted me as her life partner, in 2017, and is still with me. She is the one who has loved me, while patiently helping me to understand, assimilate and make sense of the many experiences of which I have written.

Eternal thanks go to all of the above.

"What if"

An exploration of non-material, life enhancing, Consciousness expanding and transformational, personal experiences

Foreword

For a large part of my adult life, which is quite a long time, as I could kindly be best described as 'post retirement', I have felt, in fact known, that I needed to write a book. This may be something that is quite common to many of us, which is perfectly understandable to me, because I believe we all provide a home to our inner-selves, the real 'us', which some may call our consciousness, but others may feel comfortable enough, to call our soul or spirit; I am comfortable with all of these, because they are all manmade constructs, and in my view, amount to the same thing. Whichever term we use, I am sure that many of us feel, that the real 'us' constantly seeks expression.

In my case, I have made a number of attempts to write over many years that for a variety of reasons, have failed to come to fruition. Some of those reasons have had to do with real life dynamics interrupting my creative activities. But my efforts were mainly hampered by those insidious little worms of doubt, that questioned my ability, and the relevance and validity of what was I was attempting to write. Now, please do not write me of as a delusional crank, I assure you I am not, but I now realise, that the real reason for the book remaining incomplete until now, was that intangible forces were preventing me from completing what I was attempting to write, because my attention was focussed on the mechanics of the writing process, which was possibly ego, or vanity driven, and was not focussed on the subject matter, which, with hindsight, I now see, was more important, and I now understand that initially, my efforts came to nothing, because I had been trying to write the wrong book, a book that probably would have had limited validity.

At this point, I should say that prior to beginning to write this book, I have already written, and self- published a book of Social Comment Poetry, and although it came as a real surprise that I could even write poetry, that particular ability, was never a part of my instinctive knowing that I needed to write, and I mention it only because it has a significance that you will discover, as you continue reading.

So, finally after a number of false starts, much uncertainty and many misgivings "What if." has been completed, because, it was the book that needed to be written. I hope that you find it life enhancing consciousness expanding, and totally transformational.

I am a very ordinary down to earth person, not given to fancifulness and delusion, and, I have never had the desire to sensationalise anything. I also have what I crudely call a very functional Bullshit filter that is useful in weeding out information that is simply implausible. I do not claim to have any special spiritual abilities, and I have little time for the Clairvoyants, Mediums, and Psychics that populate the stage, television and digital media, who in my opinion, are largely insincere and cynical, and pray on vulnerability and sadness. This is not the complete picture though, as there are also large numbers of sincere people, who are authentic, have genuine abilities, and an aware-ness that non–material dimensions do exist, and exert influences on our lives, that are powerful, beneficial and enriching. I recognise that much of what I have written may be difficult and challenging, and as you read on you will meet these difficulties and challenges. I can only state that what I have written is offered in truth, sincerity and love. The experiences are of course anecdotal, sadly this is the nature of these events. However, I have been at great pains to offer as much verification as possible in every case. One further point I would like to make, is that although most of us believe that science, and scientific testing methods offer absolute proof, it is rarely the case. A more accurate appraisal of what happens is that most science, certainly the quantum sciences, rather than offering absolute proof are more often based only on degree of proof. Having said all of this, I hope that everything I have written helps you to reconnect with your own possibly unspoken of experiences, and any thoughts or feelings of which you have been aware, but have been too uncertain to share with anyone else. To the less accepting, all I ask is that you read the little quotation at the start of chapter one, which came to me out of the blue, late one night, suspend your disbelief, allow yourself to become aware that the intangible does exist, and is often way more powerful than the world of everyday reality, then simply relax, and enjoy the revelations to come.

Mike Brookes.

Chapter 1

"The truth is incontrovertible, whether you believe it or not, is simply an exercise in personal choice, it will not alter truth's status one Iota".

Before I relate my story to you, I feel it may be really useful, to set aside a number of possible assumptions, misconstructions and misperceptions, to ensure that you understand that I do not have any hidden evangelical agendas, I have no desire to convert, or indoctrinate anyone into a particular practice or belief system. That would be difficult to do, as, apart from sometimes, when my children were small, taking them to the manger service at church, at Christmas, and attending the usual weddings and funerals, I do not follow, and I am not a member of any organised church or religion. While I have respect for all religious philosophies, and recognise the potency that ritual can have, I have not found, and do not seek a religion that conforms to my view of how the world works. I believe our world is both immensely mystifying and complex, and yet can be delightfully uncomplicated to live in if we choose to make it that way. I have what may be best described as a pantheistic philosophy in that I believe we all exist in a totally spiritually and infinitely connected world. Being infinitely connected, it is my belief that all our actions have an impact on everything else, in either a positive or negative manner. This indicates to me, that it is good practice to make your actions positive and peaceful, if it is your desire to live in a balanced and peaceful world. However, please do not get the impression that I am seeking a righteousness high, or being pious, piety, is the last thing I am seeking, and if I were to be told I was behaving righteously, I would probably be quite be offended, because I find righteousness can be quite unattractive. I know that we are all flawed, and I know that, that certainly includes me. I simply think it is entirely admirable that we all aspire to be better.

Although I did not have a university education, I do have a love for science, in particular, Quantum physics which drives increasingly large areas of today's technology. I think this is both a blessing and a curse, and is a subject I may touch on later. One thing that fascinates me about quantum physics is that it is all conducted in the realm of the non-material. The sub atomic particles, that we successfully manipulate to drive our digital world, can only be observed with great difficulty, because they are so infinitesimally small, that they have no material substance, they are without mass, and yet, have immense power. This is very well accepted by science, which is why I find it extremely curious, that if the principle of other non-material realms, exerting influence on everyday life experiences is raised, many, and perhaps the majority of those in the science community, would be dismissive, on the basis, that such experiences cannot be proven. However, many physicists are now coming to realise that quantum physics, and some philosophical thinking is converging. Quantum physicists are known to express the opinion that they do not know how the quantum world works, they just know how to make it work. But, this is not a lesson in science or religion and I am not equipped to give lessons on either subject. It's simply that there is a genuine contradiction between uncertainties of proof in quantum physics and the commonly experienced events that happen in the realm of the non-material, which those who experience them know to be undoubtedly true, but for which the proof may only ever be anecdotal.

I find life interesting and fascinating, and read widely, on subjects such as early pre- Christian cultures, Neuro science, Alternative Medicine, Herbalism, Eco building techniques, Green issues, Quantum Physics of course, and what is often called Frontier Science, which briefly described, are all those subjects that are at the vanguard of modern, usually non-materialist scientific thinking, that seek to identify quite how this marvellous world actually functions as it does.

I am also a practical person, and have many past times and interests. I make furniture from recycled timber, paint Watercolours, I can carve wood, tile a floor, replace a window, plaster a wall and hang a door. I have run my own businesses, trained as a Clinical Hypnotherapist, and write poetry. However, I do not want you to think I am being boastful, and I include this information simply to identify myself as a card carrying, normal, down to earth person, with his feet on the ground, not given to delusional thoughts or fantasies, and I trust that it will serve to ensure my credibility, as

I recount the consciousness expanding experiences that prompted me to write this book.

I have come to believe, that everything happens for a reason, and it is true in the case of the title for this book, and I would like to explain briefly if I may. On the wall of my summerhouse, which is warm and bright, and is a place I like to go to meditate, write, and sometimes, just chill out, is a copy of Samuel Taylor Coleridge's poem, "What if you Slept". I love it, because it asks questions about the existence of other realities that are often beyond our everyday considerations, and it encourages our imaginations to provide answers to these curious and unusual questions. It was the provocativeness of it that prompted the title, "What if?" for this book, because it begs the further question, What if What? which is inquisitive, and aligns well with the subject matter. I have included Coleridge's poem below, and I hope that you will find it thought provoking and moving. I was also, inspired to write a poem, based on the style of Coleridge's poem, that I have included at an appropriate place later in the book.

What if you Slept?

What if you Slept?
And what if in your sleep
You dreamed
And what if
In your dream
You went to heaven
And there plucked a strange and beautiful flower

And what if
When you awoke
You had that flower in your hand
Ah! What then?

Samuel Taylor Coleridge 1772-1834

Writing this book has been both challenging and interesting, and I have felt the need to give a coherent description of the unusual subject matter, in order that it would be accepted as totally sincere, and completely authentic. It has been interesting, in that, I felt compelled to write it, not primarily for my benefit, but, hopefully for what I believed it may offer others. The process has also been helpful, and informative to me, as my contemplations, have allowed me to draw the various cords of the story together, which have taken place, throughout my life, and have allowed me to reveal, what I hope is a genuine account, of the life enhancing and transformational events that I have experienced. Because of this, I now know, that our world, and the way we experience it, is much more special, and vastly different to the way we are conditioned to perceive it. In order to write this book, I have had to take a step into the unknown, not knowing what reaction to expect. But I have been privileged to have had the consciousness expanding experiences that have happened to me, and I will always feel enriched and very grateful for having done so.

This is not an autobiography, my life has been too ordinary to merit that, but there is a chronology to it that will help in recounting the events that have transformed my understanding. It is curious how things work out, because the chronology of which I talk, began with a number of interesting, but less significant events in my earlier years, through to the most powerful and transformational events, which have happened more recently, almost, as if things were meant to be this way. And, who knows that they were not?

Finally, before I move on, I would like to assure you that, although this book is about life enhancing intangible experience of a spiritual nature, which also covers the subject of death. It is not in any way, meant to be mawkish, sad or negative, in fact, I trust it will be quite the opposite, neither I hope is it weak minded and fanciful, as that would just denigrate the subject. As a Hypnotherapist, I recognise that most, if not all the problems in our lives are fear based, fear of loneliness, fear of hunger, violence, war, poverty and many more, including the strongest of all, which is the fear of death, which many of us perceive as the nothingness that awaits us at the end of our lives. All my experiences now lead me to categorically reject this belief, as will become apparent as you read on.

I believe that we should always find as much joy and humour as possible in our lives, so, I want to para-phrase, what I believe the comedian, actor, and film director Woody Allen humorously said, "I'm not afraid of dying, I just don't want to be around when it happens". From my perspective, my experiences have enabled me to feel incredibly less anxious about my eventual demise, because I am now convinced that we are all eternal. However, my apprehension remains, which is entirely normal, and for the foreseeable future, I am more than content to continue enjoying my wonderful earthbound life. I now believe that when we begin to shed fundamental fears and anxiety about death, we can begin to live life in a healthier and more joyous and fulfilling manner, which is exactly how I believe it should be.

In the following pages, you will encounter many instances that you will either find mystifying, or I hope, life changing and marvellous, possibly for some, what I have written will be met with a degree of incredulity. Other than attempting to be entirely honest, I have no control of how I will be perceived. All I can say, once more, is that the way I live and enjoy my life has been transformed by the events that I relate, and I hope it can also transform yours, so please read on, in the knowledge that it has been written with love, truth and sincerity.

Chapter 2

The delusion that we control events is ego based, and best abandoned as soon as possible. What we can do, is exercise love and truth, ensure that our feet are walking the correct path, create harmony, and leave Universal Consciousness to attend to the rest.

In 2018, I went to a Health and Wellbeing Fair in Bude, Cornwall, UK. Where bowing to what I will call affectionate but determined encouragement from my partner, I agreed, albeit reluctantly, to have a reading from one of the Clairvoyants. I have a tendency to be sceptical about readings from Mediums, in particular those found at this type of event. In the past, when I have been told by anyone about readings they have had, I have, to my shame, questioned them about whether they fed the Medium with information, or, whether the Medium was 'Cold Reading' them. Put simply, I have always been more than a little incredulous, even dismissive. But, as I had agreed to have a reading, I felt I should do it with good grace. So, I approached the lady, asked for a reading, and sat down, and without engaging in conversation, waited for her to begin. As a Hypnotherapist, I am aware of the power of language, the need for clinically clean communication, and effective listening, in order that misconstructions do not occur, and so on. While all this was running through my mind, I noticed that the Medium was looking a little nervous, until, suddenly, without asking me any questions whatsoever, she began talking. What she told me, left me totally amazed, and with my crudely expressed, but previously mentioned Bullshit filter, still perfectly intact.

What followed was incredibly revelatory and very emotional. Beginning quite tentatively, and with me deliberately saying nothing, she told me that I was in the process of writing, and that that work was interesting and valid. She went on to say that I had in fact, made a number of attempts to write a book, but had for a variety of reasons, always shelved the project. She then informed me with absolute conviction, that the writing I was engaged in at that time, would lead me back to write the book that I had shelved on a number of occasions, as that was the more important endeavour. Finally, she said that I was being helped in my present writing, by a slim lady in spirit. To close the reading, she said with complete confidence, that the book that I was to eventually write would be successful. By this time, I had tears streaming down my face, and was astonished by her accuracy. This was the first time I had ever requested a reading from a Clairvoyant, and I was really impressed by the fact that it was delivered without any prevarication whatsoever. This lady and I had not met prior to this occasion, and I purposely did not feed her, or answer any questions, and to her complete credit, she did not ask me any. I found her entirely credible and authentic. In regard to the book being successful, that statement is still prophetic, unless of course you are reading this, enjoying it, and exhorting your friends to read it too Dear Reader, in which case, I wish to thank you.

As I have said, the Clairvoyant's reading was totally accurate, and is completely verified, by the fact that at the time of the reading, I was engaged in writing what was to become a book of Social Comment poetry, entitled "Rhymes with a Reason", previously mentioned in the Foreword.

This story is worth relating in full, as it lends real credence to everything else, and may help you accept, that what you are reading is utterly authentic. A year or so prior to the event I have just related to you, my wife of well over 40 years, passed away, after two years illness with cancer. During this time, in order that she could enjoy as much light, warmth, and sunshine as possible, I built her a south facing, insulated, and heated Summerhouse. Sadly, due to the time I spent taking care of her, the building took longer to complete than I expected, and she passed away a few short weeks after it was finished. But, the building of it, kept her thinking future oriented, and she did get to use it, albeit only a few times, and loved it. Before she died, and in a shaky hand, she wrote me a two verse poem, which I cherish dearly, thanking me for building it for her. Here the story gets even deeper. Throughout the whole of our marriage, she regularly told me that she wrote poetry, while she was in that pre- waking state in the morning. Equally as regularly, I encouraged her to have a pen and notebook to hand, so that she could write them down, before they faded away forever, as the mists of sleep cleared. Because she was the type of person who was intent on getting on with the day the moment she awoke, she failed to heed my encouragement, and I had no actual proof that she could write poetry at all, until she wrote me those two verses in thanks.

Life is curious I think you will agree with me, when I tell you that, although I have always had a great love for language, and the written word, and while I had an appreciation for poetry, I had never had any poetry writing ability whatsoever. And yet, commencing early in 2018, I suddenly found myself, not just with the ability to compose poems, I became inspired, almost compelled to do so. This culminated one year later, with me, self-publishing on Amazon, having turned down an offer to publish my work, but on scurrilous terms, from a traditional publisher. During this year of almost compulsive, but really enjoyable poetry writing, often, finding myself unable to sleep, I would go downstairs in the early hours, make a cup of mint tea, and sit and write a ten or twelve verse poem. At this point I would then go to bed, sometimes as late as 3.00am, sleep like a baby, and wake entirely refreshed at the usual time in the morning. During this period, my partner and I would often remark, that we felt it was my deceased wife who was helping me to write. I have likened it to the words being downloaded through the top of my head. In the narrative to one of my poems, I wrote, "Sometimes, when I sit down to write, I have only a vague unformed idea of what I will write, until suddenly, when my pen touches the paper, the poem seems to write itself. While the poem reflects my opinions, I am otherwise unsure from where it came, but I say thank you". So, prior to having a reading from the Clairvoyant, where she not only told me all I have told you, she also told me that I was being helped by a slim lady in spirit. Obviously, the slim lady was exactly who I already presumed it was, my deceased wife, who was in actuality always a very slim person.

I know that what happened is true, and comparing what I was told by the Clairvoyant, with what I know took place, aligns so faultlessly, that it would be arrogant and cynical in the extreme of me, not to accept it entirely.

Before I leave this, I think it is worth raising a few questions, which I have considered in great depth, but I would like you to consider also, because it may help in deciding how much credence can be attached. I know what I am writing is the truth, because it is my first-hand experience, but this book has been written primarily for you, in the hope that you find it enjoyable, enlightening, and above all, life changing and believable, so my questions are:-

1. What made my partner and I go to the Health and Well-being Fair that day? When it was not something we regularly did? It was simply a random choice, on a dull and rainy day.

2. What caused my partner to almost insist that I have a reading from that specific Clairvoyant, particularly considering that she knew that I was more than sceptical of these situations?

3. In light of the fact that my partner and I had never met the Clairvoyant before, and I deliberately did not engage in any conversation with her, other than to ask for a reading, and then simply remained completely quiet, how did she manage, without asking any questions, to give me such accurate information about things that happened some weeks prior?

4. How did what she told me align so accurately with opinions I had already expressed with my partner, that I felt that I was being helped by my deceased wife? (I recognise my assumption here).

5. How did she know that I had made a number of attempts to write a book, when some of those attempts took place, not just weeks, but decades before?

6. What magic was at play, that allowed her to be discerning enough, to recognise, that I was not only writing, but enabled her to make a distinction between, and have an opinion on the value of what I was currently engaged in writing, what I had previously written, and what I would subsequently write?

It may seem that I am scrutinising this too closely, but, if we want to be believed, I think it is important that these things should withstand extreme scrutiny. While it is impossible to offer absolute proof of most things, if we exercise a desire to access verifiable truth, I believe it can be found. It will be my endeavour to ensure that everything to come will be verifiable truth.

I am not at all interested in debating, or dissecting any of what I have written with sceptical materialists, but would re-direct them to my quotation at the start of chapter 1. In order to be balanced, I would also say that they have every right to their opinions, the right to dissent, and even to be mistaken. It is my experience, that we live in a world of more than one reality, perhaps, as many scientists now believe, a world of multiple realities. I happily accept that we live in an everyday material world, while at the same time, I am aware of, and even in awe of a far more intangible, even spiritual reality, that exerts immense power over what we experience. This power from my own experience, can be comforting, keep us safe, and immeasurably enhance our human existence.

It is to our detriment, that the modern digital world, rather than increasing our awareness of a non-material reality, has a severe tendency to diminish, and even destroy it. The pace of change is now so exponential, and we are so busy assimilating change, and in fairness, also the benefits that it can bring, that we have had no time to pause, and realise that, in the process, we are losing so many of our really important human attributes, that have ensured our well-being, since we first walked the face of the earth. Our intuition and our atavistic and finely honed sixth sense, that assure our safety, that prevent us from stepping off the kerb at the wrong moment, alternatively knowing instinctively, to trust someone, you have only just met. It is a world of instincts, feelings, emotion, intuition, unspoken communication, and finely tuned senses and connection to our environment, and each other that have equipped us to be the unique human beings we are.

It is my view that, we should not consider our world as a **material, or non-material**, situation, and rather than trying to make it a case of either, **this or that**, we should accept that we live in world that values and accepts the existence of both **material and non-material** realities.

I believe that we are vastly complex, conscious spiritual beings, with hopes, dreams and aspirations, that ensure that we operate at our best, when we allow ourselves to be influenced, and guided by our positive emotions, intuitions, and instincts, knowing that the non- material dimension is an incredibly powerful reality, that inordinately enhances our lives, in more ways than we probably realise. While I recognise that the increasing influence of the digital world is inevitable, and offers many advantages, I am certain that we need to guard against its many pitfalls. I also believe that if we fail to retain, and even systematically enhance our very important human sensibilities, we may be in danger of becoming Technological Giants, as we also become increasingly spiritually diminished.

We should enjoy the warmth and connection of hearing someone's voice on the telephone, rather than through the abbreviated text messages that we think for some curious reason, is a superior and more fulfilling form of communication. We should see people if we can, rather than Emailing, texting or Face-timing/ Zooming, or whatever. We can build and enhance relationships, when we meet them in person, when we can be in contact with their aura field, when we can be aware that we chemically respond to people's physical presence, in either a good or bad way. It is a mistake, for us not to recognise the value that our massively powerful senses have in helping us navigate our way through this condition that we know as being human.

One of the great dangers of the sort of exponential change that is currently taking place, is that within a generation, the knowledge that we used to communicate in a more comprehensive and superior fashion is beginning to be lost, even to a slightly older generation than mine, while the younger generation, have no knowledge of, or ability to understand the many advantages, of reverting back to something that is better, if we so wish. I wonder how many of us, have had the experience of knowing, in a deep and spiritual sense, that we needed to be in contact with someone. Only to find, when we respond to this prompt, that the person we are contacting, is so glad to hear from us, because they really need to talk to someone, for whatever reason. I call this a cry from the heart, and it is to our benefit that we are able to be aware, and respond.

I have a very good friend, who lives about four hundred miles away from me. We worked together for eight years or so, and became firm friends. We understand and trust each other, understanding our quirks and differences very well, and feel so at ease when we talk regularly on the phone, that we can almost restart conversations we were having the previous time we spoke. All this happens despite the fact that for a number of reasons, we have not seen each other for twenty years. I cannot conceive of a relationship of this depth, beginning, and being sustained through modern digital communication methods. It is because our friendship formed through regular human connection, over many years, that the relationship continues to flourish.

"A Non-Material Otherness"

I speak of a sense of difference, of which I've forever been aware,
That renders it difficult to grasp, but has
constantly been right there.

A knowledge that's undeniable, which you
feel, but of which you can be unsure,
That life's not simply about daily routines, it's an
intuition that there's much, much more,

Not the tangible, solid and material, objects
that you can see, touch and feel,
It consists of the infinitely more ethereal, rather
than things we tend to class as 'real',

It's about a different other world, of which it's difficult to talk,
a world of the senses and intuition, when you
know the path you need to walk,

It's realising there's another realm, though
it's challenging to define,
A Non-Material Otherness, that allows our soul to know
that we have always been connected to the divine.

So, always walk a peaceful path, be aware of what's internal,
Live in tranquillity, harmony and joy, in
the knowledge that you're eternal.

Mike Brookes.

Chapter 3

When you trust enough, to state your beliefs without fear, you can be surprised that your views are reflected back to you. In this way, we can build deep mutual understanding.

I was raised in a very average, working class area, to decent but working class parents. Like many mums and dads of that generation, they were so hard put to pay the rent, keep clothes on our backs, and feed us, that if they had aspirations, they had little time, or energy for them, and certainly, didn't talk about them. As a consequence, other than feeding and clothing us, they probably had few aspirations for my four siblings and me as well. So growing up in post war Great Britain, was a fairly grey world, rather than the more brightly coloured one we live in today. Houses were uninsulated, draughty and cold, with ice on the inside of the bedroom windows in the winter when you woke up in the morning. Television, for those who had it was in its infancy, there were very few bathrooms, and the toilet, or as we correctly called it then, the lavatory, for most working class folk, was probably next to the coal house in the back yard. Despite this, I remember being happy, well fed, and having lots of freedom to play all sorts of street games with my friends. Any spiritual enlightenment that was available came through morning assemblies in the school hall with a hymn or two, a few short words from the headmaster and a prayer. Further religious education came through us being sent to Sunday school regularly. This I fear, was not because my parents wanted us to find God, but, was probably more to get us out of the house for a while on Sunday.

The first time that I remember becoming aware of a much wider and fascinating world, than the fairly mean streets that I grew up in, was when my oldest sister and her fiancé took me, unusually without any of my siblings, to the local cinema. I was around eight years old, the film was in Technicolour, was set in Kenya, Africa, and was called, "The Scarlet Spear". I have remembered the title for over well over fifty years, because it had such an impact on my young soul. Imagine my surprise when I researched it during the writing of this book, and found that it is available to watch on You-tube. I had no idea what it was about, and still, do not care. It was the magnificence of the scenery, the wild life, and the sunshine and colour that had me mesmerised, so much so, that from that day, I nourished a dream of living in Africa, which I subsequently did, and which forms part of the story to follow. Looking back, I realise that this was probably the first time I felt an aspiration for something other than what I had. It was a moment of awakening to other possibilities that was almost spiritual, and has influenced my life greatly.

My young life was generally a happy one. I loved to play, I loved to learn, and while I had plenty of friends there, I did not enjoy school, because it was rather rough, fortunately, I did not have to do much fighting in the playground, because I was good at athletics and sports, so it was unusual for me to be challenged by the school bullies. Other than always having an intuition, that I was somehow protected by an unknown force, and that life was deeper and more meaningful than the everyday events. My daily life was pleasant, and uncomplicated but otherwise, not particularly outwardly spiritual.

In writing this book, I have out of necessity looked back on my life, in an effort to catalogue, and try to understand all the events that I have experienced, that might be classed as what some would call Para Normal, but I feel comfortable calling spiritual.

There are a number of types of Para Normal, Spiritual experiences, which probably encompass the whole range of human emotions and scenarios, many of which, you will probably be aware. However, there is one experience that I struggle to categorise, but felt that I should include it anyway, as it is something that still mystifies me, and I have remembered it since I was very young. If you recall, I said earlier, that curiously, all of my experiences have happened in an incremental manner, with the seemingly less significant happening in my earlier life, increasing in significance, as my life has progressed, with the most significant, stunning and life changing occurring, thus far! most recently.

The experience that I am referring to happened when I was around thirteen years old. I had fallen very ill, with a condition that my doctor seemed unable to diagnose, in fact, he was being utterly ineffectual. I had an extremely high temperature, I was in constant and incredibly severe pain, I could not walk, I was not eating, hardly drinking, and the incessant severe pain was making me semi delirious, and preventing me from sleeping. This went on for a number of days, and the only pain relief the doctor prescribed was utterly ineffective. At the end of four days, with the pain increasing, me getting more ill and weaker, not having had more than very brief but restless sleep, my mother, got into bed at the side of me. Now, I loved my Mum very dearly, but she was not a tactile person, and did not hold me or attempt to nurse, or comfort me in any way. But almost the moment that she got into bed, my pain subsided to such an extent, that I fell very quickly into a deep, much needed sleep. Very shortly thereafter, I was hospitalised and had an emergency operation to remove an abscess in my femur, which was caused by a severe blow to my leg some months earlier. We were told after the operation, that if it had not been carried out as an emergency, I would possibly, have lost my right leg above the knee. I subsequently spent over four months in hospital being treated. I have related this event to my family, calling it the magic power of Mums. This was my first, seemingly random, inexplicable experience. I can attest to the fact that my pain left me, and I fell thankfully into a much needed sleep, beyond that, I cannot categorise it in any way. I do believe that some intangible or non-material energy was at play. It was undoubtedly a security and comfort thing, and incredibly powerful too, but, I believe it is important to acknowledge that these intangible energies come into play, at moments when they are most needed. Like most people, I accept that Mums are magic, but realistically, they probably function as conduits in these situations, so, my question is this, who or what decides to enable these non-material benevolent energies to be released? I am convinced, that there is a Consciousness that enables, facilitates and guides our existence, and that it does so, in a very timely, benevolent and life affirming manner. What that Consciousness is, I am not sure, but I do acknowledge it, and I give thanks. To simplify, I will refer to this power as Universal Consciousness, or "UC". I think that the recognition that these forces are constantly engaged in our existence, can be very enhancing to our physical and emotional state, and we should perhaps, quietly ask for these non-material energies to help us accept, and be guided by them. A final word on this experience, Scientists believe in the Placebo effect, and accept that it is powered by expectation, and perceptions. However, I did not know of placebo at the time, nor I am sure did my Mum, hence I do not believe that what happened was placebo effect, it was beyond this. As I have said previously, I am not a believer in any particular religious philosophy, but I do feel very comfortable giving simple and non- ritualised thanks. I have included a poem, titled, "My NON PRAYER", which I wrote some time ago, I hope it resonates with you.

"My Non-Prayer"

I've never been one for praying,
It's finding the words to say,
It's usually a word in gratitude,
a brief thank you for the day.

I do not become a supplicant,
And get down on my knees,

But, I offer thanks to Nature,
birds in flight, the majesty of trees.

I believe in mindfulness, in all we do and say,
Being a better version of ourselves, with every passing day,
That no wrong is ever done, with complete impunity,
if we believe in our Oneness, our absolute Unity.

Survival of the fittest, can't be allowed anymore,
That 'Might is Right', is wrong, we have to be very sure,
For, I am you and you are me, there is no separation,
Is the message for us all, Nation unto Nation.

I don't believe in worldwide revolution,
I believe in fairness, truth, and higher evolution,
To a world without hunger, war and fear,
Is an aspiration, I hold very dear.

So, in case this world should come to nought,
Precede every action with this thought,
A thought that's undeniably true,
that you are me, and I am you.

And in this way, we can measure our world,
And as we progress, as the Cosmic plan is unfurled,
We'll accept that the world is extremely abundant,
As we realise that greed and war, should now be redundant.

Chapter 4

**Everything happens for a reason, so trust,
become aware, keep watch and you will see.**

During my teenage years, typical of many young men, with plenty of testosterone to spare, in order to improve my physique, and with an idea that it would make me more attractive to any young ladies, whose eye I could catch, I began weight training with a friend, two or three times a week, after work. Hopefully, my ego did not become as inflated as I hoped my muscles were becoming. A while later through an older colleague, I became interested in Yoga. I was a young broke apprentice Printer with little money to join a club, even if there was one around. So, I got a book on Hatha Yoga from my local library, and began practicing at home in my spare time.

My life as a young apprentice Printer was a very busy one. Work began at 7.45 am. And it was necessary to be there to 'Clock On', no later than that, even by one minute, or lose fifteen minutes pay from already paltry wages. Not only that, it was quite likely you would receive a ticking off from the Foreman for your tardiness, as well. I lived six miles away from the print factory, and had to cycle there every morning, summer or winter, rain or shine, as I could not afford to go by bus, on the wage of an apprentice. The working week was 40 hours long, eight hours a day, five days a week. The work was fairly physical, and there were few opportunities to be off your feet. Being an apprentice also meant attending Night School, at least two evenings a week, until around 9.00pm. Despite all of this, most of my fellow apprentices and I thrived, but it is true to say that it was a busy life. At that time, there was the beginning of an awareness of other cultures, such as Yoga, transcendental meditation and using mind altering drugs like L.S.D. I hasten to add that, I was never into drug taking, so L.S.D. passed me by completely. But, I had read information on, what we used to call, Astral Projection, now, we would probably call it an OBE.(Out of Body Experience), and I thought that it was fascinating, but probably quite fanciful, and did not give it much further thought.

My Yoga routine, provided I had time, was done at home after work. I would stand on my head for a few minutes, which I found very easy and invigorating, and loved to do, then I would practice my Hatha Yoga, and round off the session, with a deep relaxation called 'The Corpse' posture. In order to get best benefit from this, I would ensure the room was warm, and dim all the lights before beginning. The principle of this type of deep relaxation, is really rather simple, it involves lying on the floor, hands at your sides, with palms up, heels loosely together, allowing your feet to fall comfortably apart. The rest of the instructions are about breathing, and consciously relaxing the whole of your body, while attempting to empty your mind of all thoughts.

I do not know why I found it easy to empty my mind. Some people may have said it was because there was little to empty in the first place. Or, it may have had something to do with having a very busy physical schedule, and a need to relax, or I may have had a natural aptitude for it, or all of the above, I cannot say. What is true is that I took to it, enjoyed it, and after a few days practice, was enjoying a very advanced and beneficial state of complete physical and mental relaxation, the likes of which I had never experienced before. I recall feeling a deep sense of well-being and refreshment at the end of these sessions. Looking back, I remember feeling amazed, that something so inactive, could be so invigorating and energising. Then one day, after only a week or so of practicing this routine, I had what I call my second, mystical, non-material consciousness expanding experience.

I have a continuing difficulty in finding the appropriate vocabulary, to give an adequate description for many of my experiences, because, how do you describe things that are intangible, incredibly unusual, and fall outside of the normal range of daily events, and our need to translate them into this wonderful, but sometimes totally inadequate thing that we call language. I suppose the best that I can expect, is that you will understand what my inadequate words, are attempting to describe because, you know what I am saying at a level that transcends the inadequacy of the words used.

On the day of the experience, having done my usual Yoga routine, I began my deep relaxation routine, and dropped very quickly into a completely relaxed physical and mental state, becoming entirely unaware of my human form. I could not feel the pressure of my body on the carpeted floor, my heartbeat, my breathing, or any need to adjust my position for comfort, I was simply aware of my mind very slowly turning over, independent of my corporeal form. When, in an instant, without being aware of the transition, I realised that I was looking down on the body that I lived in, lying utterly motionless and apparently lifeless, on the floor below me. This did not disturb me in any way at all, because, at the same time that I was above my inert form, I recognised, that I was in a non-physical state, in a non-physical realm. There was no feeling of being confined by being in the building that was my home. I felt light, free and happy, without an Iota's concern for my body, because I knew with absolute certainty, that I was the entity that was me, not the motionless form lying below me.

In recalling what I prefer to call my O.B.E. (Out of Body Experience), rather than the outdated term, Astral Projection. I am impressed that my level of recall, and that the emotions attached to it are so complete. I felt liberated, and at one with everything, knowing that all was exactly as it should be, and would be. It is curious though, that I have little recollection of re-entering my physical form, other than my eyes opening and having a sense of being extremely relaxed, and energised, with a quiet sense of elation and positivity that our lives happen in more than one reality, and that I had had the privilege of this consciousness expanding experience. It is this that sits at the foundation of my certainty, that we are conscious spiritual beings that are allowed to experience life on earth through our physical, but mortal bodies. However, I also believe that through Mindfulness, Meditation, and practices like Yoga, Qigong and Tai chi, etc. we can learn to connect with our spiritual selves. It is becoming accepted, that emotional/spiritual well-being, is paramount in maintaining our physical health. I have read information written by an eminent Neuro scientist, who is of the opinion that as much as eighty per cent of physical disease, or dis-ease, can have its genesis in our mental/emotional state. So we should think of our health as being both spiritual and physical, and endeavour to care for both.

Perhaps we should always take note, when someone says, "Be kind to yourself", or "Be gentle with yourself", and just do exactly that. Here is a simple example of what I am trying to explain. Anxiety, which is an emotional state, causes the release of the stress hormone Cortisol, which is a physical manifestation, of the emotional stress we are feeling. This anxiety can be picked up by those with whom we share our lives, who can also, then begin to feel troubled and anxious, releasing stress hormones of their own. So, stress, can be contagious, along with ultimately causing long term physical illnesses to ourselves, which stress engenders. It is therefore, important that we remember, that we live in an infinitely connected world, and as such, everything we do affects the world around us, to a greater degree than we imagine, so the principle of enhancing our spiritual and physical lives, by being kind to ourselves, and everyone else, serves also to enhance the well-being of everyone, including ourselves.

We are dual beings, with a physical body, and a non-physical self, whether you wish to call it spirit, soul, or ethereal entity, is immaterial, (please excuse the pun), they are simply man made constructs, devised to help us understand something that is for some, hard to define. I am convinced that the more we accept, and practice living as dual beings, who can have an immense beneficial impact on the world in which we live, the better everyone's lives will become. I do not believe I am being naïve, by having this belief. To the doubters, I would simply say, that until you have tried to facilitate change in this way, doubt is simply an unproven opinion that only has validity after the effort to change has been attempted, at which point it will become a certainty that you have either succeeded, or failed. What I do believe everyone would agree with, including the doubters, is that there is more than adequate proof that our present paradigm is not working.

There is a state called Negative Security, which involves desiring change, but continuing to do familiar things that are nevertheless comfortable but do not work, on the futile assumption that eventually they will. When the simple answer is, if something is not working, and you want positive change, begin immediately, to do something that you feel will bring it about. I find it curious that we humans hold onto behaviours that palpably do not work, when rats, for instance, will quickly give up patterns of behaviour that do not work, for ones that do. The American phrase, "Go Figure", comes to mind.

Something that has occurred to me, as I continue writing about these wonderful and often inexplicable events, which appear to have sequence and reason, is that they did not happen to a plan of my devising. I did not wake up one day, and say to myself. "I am going to ensure that I have a series of revelatory and inexplicable experiences in my life". And yet I did! I continue to be amazed, and say thank you.

Chapter 5

When you set aside your resistance to the belief that the world functions in ways that are marvellously baffling yet have the appearance of verifiable truth, you can begin to see the magic.

After finishing my apprenticeship, and marrying in 1969, I was becoming more and more dissatisfied with my job, which was not the career choice to which I was best suited. I found life in the UK somewhat stifling, and un-exciting. So, I began casting around for an adventure, and new opportunities. As you can imagine my thoughts turned to fulfilling my long held dream of seeing Africa. It's curious, that if you set the intention for something, you can, if you are prepared to be aware, realise that the Cosmos, or whatever term you are comfortable with, is listening and responding. So, in order to be proactive, I obtained the address of a large printing company in Kenya, from a trade magazine, who advertised positions fairly regularly, for printers in the UK, to take up positions over there. Although, Kenya was my first choice, I discovered that they were not recruiting at that time. I was disappointed, but resolved to carry on looking for opportunities elsewhere in Africa. When I read an advertisement in the following month's trade magazine, for one position in the Republic of South Africa, I applied for it, went for the interview, and was offered the job, at double the amount I was earning in the UK, in a system where income tax was only ten percent, as opposed to over twenty percent in the UK.

After overcoming my wife's initial resistance to leave her Mum and siblings, and making her understand that my dream of living in Africa had been with me, since my sister and her fiancé took me to see that film set Kenya, a matter of seventeen years or so ago, when I was just a boy, that she agreed, and about five weeks later, we left for the Republic of South Africa. Of course, there was soul searching to be done for many reasons. It has to be remembered, that we were very young, and very green. Neither of us had ever flown before, I had never been further than the Isle of Wight, and my wife was even less travelled than me. There was also the problem, that at the time, South Africa was an Apartheid state, and we had to assimilate that and how that sat with our consciences. We rationalised it, by telling ourselves that the opportunity was too good to miss, we were not racists, and we were not going there to personally oppress anyone. We knew Apartheid was wrong, and before leaving, we decided that we would not be prepared to employ anyone as domestic staff, as was very common at the time. But this subject is huge, and this is not the forum for dealing with it now. Suffice it to say, that the reality was, and still is very complex, and we found things way different to our expectations. In fact, we discovered that English people were very well liked by most of the ethnic African races. Both my wife and I were pleased to see apartheid dismantled, along with minority white rule. My very final word on this is, that it saddens me, that South Africa and its people have still not achieved its potential for most of the indigenous population, with segregation being done based on wealth and not race. It could be argued however, that segregation based on wealth, occurs pretty much world-wide, including Europe but once again, this is not the appropriate forum for this discussion.

I remember leaving the UK with a heavy cold, in the middle of winter, having packed and shipped our meagre possessions in one small packing crate. We had only been married about six months, and we left the country with only thirty pounds to our name, feeling excited and full of hope.

Africa has a smell that is unmistakeable and very difficult to define, there is warmth and a dryness, to the air you breathe, and the sun, which sits higher in the sky, has a very special quality too, and without being fanciful, I always felt that Africa pulses with a special energy, at the same time that it teems with myriad, and diverse life forms. From the moment we landed, we were blown away by the experience, and were doubly pleased, when we arrived in Natal, (I believe, presently called Kwa Zulu), where we were going to live, which has possibly the best climate in the whole of Africa, and the most beautiful and majestic scenery anyone could wish for.

The next inexplicable event happened a few months later, when we had rented a house on a small farm, about five miles out of the town of Pietermaritzburg. When we decided to get married, prior to leaving the UK, we chose a pair of wedding rings, from a Jewellers in our home town, that were made by an apprentice Goldsmith, as his final exam pieces. They were an obvious pair, as they were highly decorated and very similar but not identical, and we were very proud to have them, to identify our recently married status. On one Saturday morning, we had done the clothes washing, and were pegging it out on the washing line, when suddenly my wife let out a surprised cry, and said her wedding ring had flown off her finger into the grass. The ring had become loose, because she had lost weight, and we had not yet, had it re-sized. The other problem was, that the grass, which had grown quickly, was about a foot high, and her ring had disappeared into it, but we did not know where. We were really distraught about it, particularly my wife, as the rings, being 'one offs', were not replaceable. So we both searched the whole area on hands and knees, incredibly thoroughly for well over an hour, cutting the long grass by hand as we searched, without finding it, even though we believed that our search area must have been large enough. As you may imagine, this was well before the advent of metal detectors. The rest of the day we were very unhappy about it, and went to bed that night, still feeling very disturbed.

In my pre-waking state, early the next morning I had a dream that I would find the ring in a very specific place, a place where no-one would have ever perceived it could be. What I do know, is that I woke the next morning, knowing exactly where I would find it, the certainty was so strong, that I leapt straight out of bed, pulled on a pair of shorts, and headed into the garden. My wife came awake at my haste, and started to ask what on earth I was doing. I had to ask her rather brusquely, not to delay me, telling her I needed to do something, and on this, I ran out of the house into the garden. I knew that if I engaged in conversation with her, that the dream would fade away. Needless to say, within what could have been no more than a minute, at the very most, two, I had found the ring in the exact place that I had dreamt it would be. My wife was overjoyed, and amazed that I had not only found it, but where I had found it, which left her speechless. The ring remained on her finger for the rest of our very long married life. This story, is obviously an anecdotal, and a seemingly, simple one. On the face of it, I agree. I know that many people have apparently prophetic dreams, and that some of them are fanciful, possibly even delusional, such as dreaming the winning lottery numbers, and do not become fact. However, some dreams do become fact, as was the case with me finding my wife's ring. In reference to metal detecting, should they have been available, without sweeping a whole area that was outside the perceived area where we assumed the ring was lost, we would still have failed to find it. So, I now believe that my dream was the most efficient method of it being recovered, and that a "Consciousness" was responsible for it.

I would like to share my thoughts with you about this event, and I realise that once again, I am possibly being over analytical, but, if there is no truth, the story loses all its power. At the time of my life that this happened I was young, and relatively unformed in terms of my beliefs and philosophies. I had no expectations of dreaming anything specific, least of all, being guided to find lost rings by them. I thought dreams were largely random events that were often difficult to understand, because they usually made little sense. So, I would not have had any preconceived expectations, even about having dreams at all, let alone being accurately guided by them. What makes this experience so meaningful to me is that I could have shrugged the dream off as some sort of aberration, and eventually tried to replace my wife's ring with as close a facsimile as possible. Instead, I felt compelled to hurry out of bed, guided by the dream to find it in an area where it seemed inconceivable it would be. In short, I did not will this to happen, all I did in my youthful naivety was to respond to the prompting of a very propitious dream.

I have since had portentous dreams that, once again, I was not seeking, or expecting, that have been verifiably true, about more important events, which I will relate later. All I can say, at this point, is that there does not seem to be an explanation for this event, it is mystifying. Could it be therefore, that there is a Consciousness that intercedes, always benevolently, that we usually fail to acknowledge, or of which, we are not usually aware?

I endeavour not to live in a world where I fabricate things in order to convince myself that the world is magic, quite the opposite in fact. However, all of my un-looked for experiences, have allowed me to observe first hand, that there does appear to be benevolent intervention in events, and I find that mystifying, and even magical.

In the next chapter, I will relate an event that has held enormous significance to me ever since it happened, and still has the power to completely baffle me.

Before moving on to the next chapter however, I would like to tell you about one of the most beautiful week-ends we had while in South Africa, because it may just give you a sense of how magical it was, and I would like you to understand that it was a very earthly, but nevertheless, spiritual experience. Within a year or so of arriving in South Africa, we had our first child, a little girl, who we named Louise. When she was around three months old, we were asked to take a trip to the Drakensberg mountains and stay in a game ranger's hut near the top, just below the near vertical rock escarpment into Lesotho, formerly Basutoland, which was an independent mountain nation, within the borders of South Africa. The friends who had asked us were friends from our hometown in the UK, who had moved to South Africa around the same time as us. Of course, we were mad keen to go, and although it involved a two and a half hour car journey, some of it on unmade dirt roads, which would take us to the Natal Parks Game Ranger's house. Then a seven or eight mile trek on a contour path up the mountain, before reaching the overnight dwelling. We said yes, we would go. Looking back on it, I have to shrug and think about the impetuosity of it, and the possible danger, not to ourselves so much, but to Louise. However, we had considered all of this, in the way young, strong, fit, resourceful people will do, and, I am happy to report that it went perfectly well.

The walk up the mountain was wonderful, the mountain air was probably the purest we had ever breathed and the day was warm, even very warm, sunny and dry. There were five of us, three men, and two women, and we all had backpacks, and in my case, I also had a papoose strapped to my front, with Louise comfortably enjoying the ride. At three months old, it was no hardship to carry her, until we had to cross a beautifully clear mountain stream that was bridged by two tree trunks, and a hand rail that was trying its best to fall over, so it was no help at all. Also one of the trunks had warped severely, so it dipped about a foot below the other one, which made walking across it quite tricky. So, we unstrapped Louise, took her across separately, and went back for the packs, after taking a break, and fooling around in the water, before we recommenced our walk up the mountain.

The journey was really enjoyable. Once we had lost sight of the Game Ranger's hut, we did not see a road, or hear any traffic, there were no fences and no telegraph poles, and the only person we saw, was a horse mounted Zulu ranger coming down the mountain, after preparing the hut for our overnight stay. We saw baboons some distance away, that became a bit disturbed by us, and got a bit fractious, until they realised that we did not represent a threat. There were Proteas, South Africa's national flower growing at numerous places, and we walked past a number of Cape Eland, (one of the largest of antelopes), who were absolutely indifferent to us, although we passed within thirty feet or so of them. Other than a mist coming down, for a short while, before we reached the hut, the walk was beautiful, safe, and entirely enjoyable.

On reaching the hut, we attended to Louise, who had been totally content throughout, then, prepared dinner, for which we were very ready, after which, we relaxed for a while. Sunset, which is very fleeting, is rarely later than early evening, depending on the time of year, and where you are. So, later in the evening, after enjoying a warming brandy, we went outside to look at the night sky. In the developed world, due to light pollution, from human habitation, industry, street lighting etc. access to truly dark skies, is very hard to find, because of it, many of us rarely, if ever, see how spectacular the night sky is, in clear weather, with zero light pollution, we did that night, and it was stunning. Rather than looking at the usual major constellations of stars, seemingly alone with massive spaces in between, the sky was absolutely teeming with more stars than you could imagine. As the younger generation may say these days, "It was epic!" However it is described, that experience alone was worth the walk up the mountain. When I was in my early teens, a friend and I would disappear into the Derbyshire Peaks when we could, and we camped under some fairly light pollution free skies, but, I have never experienced such a perfect night sky as this.

The next morning we awoke just as the sun was rising, and we went outside to greet the day. I have never seen a more spectacular sight, than standing at the top of that mountain, with no roads in sight, no road noise, no aircraft, no fencing, or electricity pylons, literally no sign of man's intrusion into the landscape at all. And the only horizon was below us down the mountain, where the sun was just beginning to burst over the landscape, to spread its light and warmth over everything before it. It was truly spectacular! After breakfast, in glorious weather, we made our way happily and uneventfully, down to our cars, at the Ranger's house. The experience had been both a physical and spiritual one that we were privileged to have, and it has remained a cherished part of the landscape of my life ever since.

In revisiting this event, it has occurred to me that we were all totally 'off-grid', although that was not a term that was used then, for the whole of that week-end. I was relatively used to going camping, and being 'off-grid', to use today's terminology, to the extent that the nearest phone box was some miles away. However, this was before mobile phones and the internet, and we were all around seven thousand miles away from our parents in the UK and, some of them did not have telephones anyway, so we had to keep in touch with them by writing letters. The astonishing thing is that rather than feeling vulnerable and isolated, I felt liberated by the beauty, the wildness and most of all, the isolation. The curious thing is that it was never even a topic of conversation between us on that week end we simply accepted it as normal. I wrote earlier about the negative effect that the digital world is having on society. Maybe, as the story I have just related indicates, we can learn something, by reminding ourselves that we were able to live very fulfilled and even enhanced complete lives, in a different, but possibly more connected way, without digital technology. In 2019, I wrote a poem about this, a shortened version of which I have included below. I hope it explains how I feel about this subject.

Put the Genie back in the Bottle

Our world needs re-balancing if you look you'll clearly see,
That it needs much more, than our reliance on technology,
Yes, Medical Technology can heal the sick,
sometimes make people whole,
But in the midst of all the science, we should not forget the soul.

We can build computers, that calculate to the Nth degree,
We've developed Social Networks that allow us all to see
friends and family, wherever they are, it really doesn't matter,
we can contact them on WhatsApp, and have a good old natter.

Or, we can automate our phone systems,
so there's no need to converse,
So that as people, we don't connect, it really is perverse,

We can set a course for Venus, explore the deepest ocean,
we can measure the size of the Universe,
but we still have little notion,

Of how to solve the problems that beset us every day,
we're swift to engage in thoughtlessness,
and when there's blame to lay,
we can get red faced and angry, gesticulate and shout,
or, walk away in a frightful Huff! What's that all about?

So, don't take your anger to Facebook, or its little cousin Twitter,
To let the whole world and his brother, know you're feeling bitter,
If people begin pushing you don't push back, just wait,
Make your heart peaceful, and their anger will dissipate,

It seems we've opened up a version, of the fabled Pandora's Box,
We've swung the lid right open, and thrown away the locks,
That children are dying because of the Internet, really is bizarre,
I'm now entirely convinced, that technology's gone too far,

We need to pause, take a deep breath
our behaviour is now insane,
before our Social Media obsession drives
our culture down the drain,
we should value systems we had before,
ease back on technology's throttle,
and enjoy the things we hold dear from yesteryear,
Put the Genie back in the Bottle.

Chapter 6

**There are two ways to be fooled. One
is to believe what isn't true;
The other is to refuse to believe what is true.
Philosopher: SOREN KIERKEGAARD.**

We enjoyed our time in South Africa, but at the end of a five year stay, and having had two children, (we now had a son, Matthew, around a year old), we made an impromptu decision to return to the UK which is a decision I have had doubts about many times, because Africa still remains embedded deeply in my soul. But then, I have come to recognise that all things happen for a reason, and now, I just try to be aware, because I know that I usually find out in due course.

The next and very powerful experience had its genesis in Jan Smut's Airport in Johannesburg, as we were preparing to embark onto the flight back home. It was a big undertaking, as it was a long flight with two small children, and although we were committed to returning, we were naturally apprehensive about our course of action. I was just in the moment, getting on with the process, when my wife paused, and suddenly exclaimed, that she had a bad feeling about the flight. At which point I began asking questions about her having changed her mind about leaving etc. and she told me no, but she knew there was going to be a problem with the aircraft, which was a Jumbo-Jet. I do not like flying, and went into panic mode, asking all sorts of questions, such as, what did she mean, how did she know, what did she think was going to happen, and so on, finally saying, that I was not going to take us onto the plane, with two small children if we were in danger. I was extremely worried and so disturbed, that I repeated that we would have to miss the flight, and take the next one. To me, this was a self and family preservation moment. We were having this intense conversation for quite some time, with me prepared to do anything but get on the flight. Until, suddenly, with total certainty, she told me that although she was sure there was going to be a problem with the plane, it was OK, we could get on the flight, we were not going to die or be injured. She did not know what the problem was going to be, but we would not be hurt. Having received these assurances, and despite my remaining misgivings, we boarded the flight to Jomo Kenyatta Airport in Nairobi, Kenya, East Africa, where would refuel.

I should say at this point, that my wife was a very down to earth person, (excuse the unintentional pun), she was not given to fancifulness, or dramatics and she lived her life in a very practical way, neither having the time, or the inclination for anything like predicting future events. For this reason, I trusted her entirely when she did so. I also trusted her word, when she finally told me we were safe to board the plane. Once we had taken off, and our attention was on attending to the children, I gradually began to settle down and felt a little better. Later having landed in Kenya and refuelled, we once again took off into the dark African night without incident. However, as we continued to climb, it became obvious that we had taken off into a typical African thunderstorm, complete with deafening thunderclaps, high wind, torrential rain, and a literally awesome display of forked lightning. We had experienced such storms while living in South Africa, and used to enjoy the raw natural power and spectacle of them, plus the fact that they would eventually pass over, the sun would come out, the ground would steam for a brief period, as it dried, and life would return to normal. 21

In this case, life did not return to normal very quickly at all. We became aware that the plane was being severely buffeted by the storm, and we could see the display of pyrotechnics through the windows, so everyone was extremely ill at ease, when suddenly, there was a particularly bright lightning flash, and the plane rocked, before it corrected itself. We realised something was amiss, when there was a sudden surge of activity from the stewards, removing all obstructions from the emergency doors. The captain then announced over the intercom that we should put our shoes on, fasten our seat belts, and keep our children awake. He then calmly informed us that one of the engines had been struck by lightning, which had disabled it, and while we could continue with the flight, powered by the remaining engines, the protocol was that we should return to the nearest airport, which was Nairobi, for repairs to be carried out, and we would be put aboard a different flight.

I think everyone felt a little easier at hearing that we were not about to hurtle to our doom somewhere in Africa. But, any feelings of relative safety, were quickly dispelled, when he went on to say that, although this was the plan, we could not do so immediately, because having just refuelled, we were too heavy to land, and we needed to circle the Airport for thirty minutes, in order to jettison enough fuel, to ensure that we did not catch fire on landing. Ordinarily, I would have been relatively comfortable with that, had it not been for the fact that we were about to pump massive volumes of highly inflammable jet fuel, into the midst of a huge amounts of fork lightning as we did so. Thankfully, after about half an hour, the excess jet fuel was jettisoned safely, and we re-landed in Nairobi slightly fraught, but otherwise physically safe. The process of transferring to another flight was interminable, but eventually, we were transferred, and returned without further incident to Heathrow, London. Although I was a nervous flyer, because the incident which my wife had predicted had now happened, I boarded the replacement flight totally without misgivings.

I have thought about this many times, since it happened all those years ago, in order to understand by what mechanism my wife could not only have known that there was going to be a significant problem with the aircraft, but have also, been completely certain, that despite this, it was safe for us to board the plane with our young children and take the flight, and we would not be harmed. Added to this, she not only entirely accurately predicted it, she did so before even getting on the aircraft, also predicting an event that would take place half a continent away, and many hours in the future. The fact that she did this, while dealing with the 'nuts and bolts' matters, such as attending to children, manipulating luggage, and ensuring we had the necessary paperwork and so on, is astonishing. When I wrote above, the phrase, 'by what mechanism', I do not believe for a moment, that there was any mechanism involved at all. I rather believe that there was a Consciousness involved, and that Consciousness, what I now call (U.C.) was making us aware, through my wife, not some vague signal that something was going to occur, it was far more specific than that; because other than identifying the details, we were informed that (a) a problem would arise, and (b) we would be safe. As is usual, the whole of this is anecdotal, and the sceptics and other such Naysayers, may pour scorn if they so wish. I would refer them to the quotation at the beginning of this paragraph by Soren Kierkegaard, while I express my humble gratitude, and continue to believe that we live in a world where intangible, non-material forces, exert a benevolent influence on our lives, whether or not we believe in them.

Chapter 7

The Universe begins to look more like a great thought than like a great machine.
PHYSICIST and ASTRONOMER, JAMES JEANS

Having returned from South Africa, the ensuing years in the UK were given over to raising children, of which we finally had four, two girls and two boys, establishing a good home, and making our way, in a work a day world. I was always a very hands-on parent, and was never happier than when I was teaching my kids to ride a bike, swim, pushing them on a swing, or having all sorts of adventures, and showing them how to do the myriad things that children need to do, in order to learn how to navigate through life. So, my life was more about paying the mortgage, mowing lawns, decorating the house, and living in the moment, than seeking spiritual enlightenment. These middle years are probably typical of many people's lives, in that everything is about the dynamics and reality of life, and I was for the most part, happy with it that way. As I have said before I was more of a man of action, rather than being someone given to being 'otherworldly' and contemplative.

It was during this part of my life, that I became a Watercolour artist. This was really fulfilling for me, because, although at thirteen, I eventually passed a scholarship to attend an Art school, I never rated my abilities, and had not painted anything in the intervening years, except walls, doors, and skirting boards. It's curious, when you become aware, how things happen when it is time for them to take place. Other than getting on with daily life, and, in quiet moments asking myself existential questions about the reason or purpose for life, and intuitively knowing that there was a meaning to it all, my life was about living in the dynamics of the moment. Like many other people, I had moments of precognition, intuition and so on, other than that my life was filled with joy, anxiety, concern, fun, humour and the daily routine, with little or none of the transformational experiences that were to come.

Something I am now aware of is that "U.C". informs, controls, and guides our lives, but will at times remain quiet and inactive, and allow us to simply be, until it is needed once again. Looking back, I am entirely certain that my poetry writing ability is a thing that was given to me, and controlled by forces beyond myself. Following my initial months of writing poetry almost compulsively, the writing stopped as immediately as it began, and during that time, I did not, nor could write a word. Then, a year later, around the beginning of June 2020, I started writing again, not because I decided consciously to do so, but because suddenly, I felt compelled to do so again, because the poems were simply there ready to be written. During a three month period, I wrote more than twenty poems. This stopped abruptly in early September, as the words, and once again, the compulsion just left me. This was worrying at first, until I realised that it will return as it did before, and September 2020, was when I began writing this book, the book that has been in gestation for many years, and was predicted by the Clairvoyant discussed earlier. Was this my decision? I know what I believe, and I am content for you to interpret as you wish Dear Reader. A very similar thing happened with my art work. For around ten years, I was inspired to paint very regularly and enjoyably, with some success.

This was one of the reasons for moving to Cornwall, as many of my paintings were inspired by holidays here. It was my intention to spend much of my time pursuing more success as a painter of Cornish harbour scenes, in my adopted county. Has this happened? No! Since moving here in early 2000, I have not completed one watercolour. Some would possibly be upset by this, but it does not upset me at all. Painting enhanced my artist's eye for texture, colour, light and shade, and the beauty of my surroundings, all of which were a great addition to my life. Now, I simply accept that the decision was not mine to make. I did have that intention, but I am learning to accept that when what I call Consciousness, Spirit, or to paraphrase the quotation at the start of this chapter, the "Great Thought" decides something different for you, just show gratitude and go for the ride.

One more interesting thing that I would like to include from this period of my life is that I became interested in and practised Qigong for ten years. Once again, it was a random item on the radio that was the genesis of my interest. I believe that I heard the item for a reason, as it was on radio four, which was not a station that I usually listened to, but did on this particular day. Qigong can simply be described as a non-combative form of martial art. It is obviously a form of exercise and movement which can be beautiful to see (except when I do it!) and is very beneficial, physically and mentally. It enables strength and vitality to be built through Qi, or Chi in the body's meridians, which are largely dismissed by western medical science. I have no conclusive proof whether western medical science is right or wrong, all I can say, is I believe and have experienced Qi energy, and it is very real.

A humorous tale regarding this is that my youngest son, who was a six footer of around seventeen at the time, came in as I was finishing a Qigong session one day, and was looking for a bit of horse play, which was fine with me, so I said OK, but you will not be able to move me. This was met with the usual verbal bragging of a seventeen year old, with him saying things like, "Of course I will old man", and so on, which was all part of the fun. I responded by saying "Alright, just give me a second to engage my 'Chi' energy and try to lift me, move me, or push me over" When I told him to start, he could not move me in any way, it was like I was rooted into the earth. This was really funny, and surprising, because, I had no idea that I would be able to resist his efforts, and curiously, as soon as I released my concentration, and told him to try again, he lifted me easily off my feet. We repeated this silliness a number of times, and providing I was locked down as I called it, his efforts were all in vain. I suppose many of us have seen this trick done by Illusionists on the television, and possibly wondered how it is done. Well, I inadvertently found out, and it caused amusement in the family. This is not a serious point, but if I were asked if I believe in Qigong, and 'Chi' energy, I would definitely say yes. This is not seriously spiritual stuff, but it was surprising, and fascinating, and is an indication that there is such a thing as the non-material, and it is immensely powerful. Looking back on it, I wonder whether I was supposed to practice Qigong in order to realise this. Other than the fun, and the enhanced wellbeing it gave me, I still wonder quite where "Chi energy" comes from.

Chapter 8

We are not on the outside looking in, everything that we think and do, is connected to and influences everything in the Universe. We continuously create our world moment by moment.

Having moved to Cornwall, our lives obviously went through a number of changes. Once again it is curious how life happens in ways that you do not anticipate. My sister had lived in Cornwall for many years having met a Cornishman who was living in our home town, because his father had moved to our town to marry a local lady, my sister married the Cornish-man, and they subsequently moved back to Cornwall. My mother, after the death of my father, had subsequently remarried, and moved to Cornwall to be near to my sister. My youngest daughter had also met a Cornishman living in our town in the midlands, married him, and they had also moved back to Cornwall. We followed them, within a few weeks, which we had planned to do for many years, together with our youngest son, finally being followed by our oldest son and his family, a few months later. So, there is an indication that there were a number of connections occurring, that could perhaps be happenstance, but may be something more than that. I simply see the many connections and wonder.

About ten days after moving to Cornwall, my lovely mum died. She was just a few days away from her ninety second birthday, with seemingly no health issues. She was as sharp as a very sharp tack, and had a very naughty sense of humour. Her death came as a real shock, because it was unexpected. She died of an aortic aneurism, became quickly unconscious, and died within fifteen minutes of becoming unconscious. If there is such a good thing as a good death, I suppose that came pretty close, for which, I was thankful for her.

Mum was not wealthy, but she left me and my siblings a small amount each, in her Will. Again, connections occur when least expected. A short while after mum's demise, I was driving alone in my car, feeling a little sad, and once more, curiously, listening to the radio, when I heard an item that set me on a new course in my life. The programme was discussing the subject of Hypnotherapy, which was very well presented, as it dispelled the popular myths and misperceptions that have been propagated around the subject, instead it presented it as the very powerful form of therapy it is. Sadly, it is still a very much maligned and under recognised therapeutic system. However, it appealed to me, and having Mum's bequest, I could afford to enrol on a two year certification course, in order to be qualified to practice as a Clinical Hypnotherapist. Other than being beneficial to others, it enhanced my understanding of how the mind functions, and quite how complex and interconnected our emotional system is. Studying Hypnotherapy lead me to reading widely about Neuroscience, which subsequently lead me to being instrumental in what is the most transformational event that propelled me to write this book, and has completely enhanced my life, fundamentally altering everything I believe. I know that when I write about it you will immediately understand why this is so, and I sincerely hope that it has the same transformational and beneficial effect on you.

Chapter 9

We spend much time with our psychic senses switched off, until Universal Consciousness insists that we switch on our receivers, pay attention, and act on information received.

Moving to Cornwall meant that professionally, I was not only leaving many very loyal customers, who over the years, had also become valued friends, I was also leaving my job, which I had really enjoyed doing. There were also our neighbours of twenty one years, who were friends as well, and being the same age as us, we had raised our children together. Then there were our friends, some of whom, other than our sojourn in South Africa, we had known since childhood. So the move represented a big change in all of our lives, and the people who populated it.

My next experience concerns one such person I had known since we were both sixteen years old apprentice printers working for the same company. His name was Mick, and although we were very different personalities, we always got along well, and despite our paths diverging, over the years, we always found it enjoyable and mutually beneficial, to maintain consistent, if periodic contact through business. It could be said, that, although we were never bosom buddies who spent leisure time together, in truth we were both probably too busy, but we held each other in mutual high regard, and found each other comfortable company. This was another relationship that, for a number of years, was not sustained when we moved, and my working life took a different route entirely. Although we did not intend to neglect the relationship, it simply happened because I was very busy establishing a new life in Cornwall. I had not forgotten about him, but it would be honest to say that for around three years or so, he had not been in the forefront of my mind, and we had had no contact whatsoever, until I suddenly began having dreams concerning him.

These dreams were powerful and portentous, and contained the disturbing news that he had died. Curiously, it was not like the dream I had about where to find my wife's wedding ring, which came to me as I awoke early in the morning, and I knew that I needed to act, before the message was lost. In this dream, I was more aware that I was having the dream as I slept, and what it was telling me. What I also found very different, was the fact that this dream did not fade from my memory at all, as the mists of sleep cleared, it remained entirely clear throughout the day. Despite this, having told my wife about it, who was aware of my long standing connection with him, and that the dream had had a disturbing effect, I finally shrugged it off, and telling myself it was an anomaly, I put it to the back of my mind, and then got on with my day.

The following night, the same dream with the same portentous message was repeated. Feeling even more disturbed, I discussed it with my wife, but once more, pushed it to the back of my mind. This scenario was repeated, with all the same detail for the following two nights, making a total of four consecutive nights, having exactly the same dream. By this time I knew that I needed to investigate, as by now, I was entirely certain that the dream would persist every night, until I did. Obviously, I found this quite traumatic, as I knew it needed to be handled with sensitivity. I was fortunate in this, because I had known his receptionist for many years. So I rang Mick's company number, with my heart in my mouth and asked to speak to him. You can imagine my relief, when the receptionist greeted me in her usual pleasant way, and said, "Yes, of course you can Mike, hold on I'll put you through".

At this point, I breathed a huge sigh of relief, and a lot of the anxiety drained away, as it was now obvious he had not died at all, and I began to wonder what had caused such mistaken but persistent dreams.

It then became a question of how I would open the conversation with him. You have to bear in mind that we had not spoken for more than three years, and although he knew we were leaving, I still felt the awkwardness of the situation. So, having greeted each other, I simply came right out with it, and said something to the effect of. "I had to phone you because, for the last four nights, I've dreamt about you". This seemed the most innocuous way to begin the conversation. Now, anyone who knows me knows that while I may be spiritual, and not outwardly an Alpha male, I am a confirmed heterosexual. What you also need to know, is that he is also entirely heterosexual, and he can on occasion, also have a very schoolboy, but deadpan wit. So I was not in the least surprised, when not batting an eyelid, he replied by asking, in the least "Camp" voice you can imagine. "I hope you weren't having carnal knowledge of me were you?" Thankfully, I was quick enough witted to fire back with. "No Mick I don't think you're ever going to get that lucky". At which point, our joint humour, smoothed the way for the rest of the conversation to be held.

When we eventually put our silly schoolboy humour aside, I went on to tell him that the dreams I had been having were powerful and persistent, and were informing me that he had died. I told him that I had initially been disturbed, and then shrugged the experience off, until the same dream recurred consecutively over four nights, at which point, I knew that I had to investigate. On hearing this, his tone became serious, and he informed me that he was obviously still alive and well, but, unfortunately his partner of many years, a lady I had had dealings with, who was also his business partner, had died suddenly, a matter of only a few days before my dreams started. I was shocked to hear this and offered my sympathy and we talked about it, but although Mick was obviously upset, he tended to hide his deeper feelings, so I was uncertain how hard her death hit him. Curiously, this sad event served to renew our connection with each other, and I have kept in touch with him by phone on a regular basis, ever since that dream occurred, which is over fifteen years ago. I have done so, because I have had an intuitive feeling that I was supposed to. Also, it did occur to me, that in future, it would occasionally be good to receive news by a more conventional route.

I am blessed with a good memory that seems particularly powerful in recalling these experiences, for which I am grateful, because, as I have said before, if there is no truth, then, relating such things would be futile. The experience, as usual, leaves me pondering quite how and why these things work as they do, and I have listed them below.

Mick and I were not in contact with each other at the time of the dreams, and he was not at the forefront of my mind, so, why did I dream of his death, and not his partner's.?

Although I knew Mick's partner, and we dealt with each other occasionally, we did not have the sort of relationship that may have indicated that I needed to know of her demise via dream.

I understand that the dreams were relevant to the situation, but I wonder why they were about Mick's death, and not his partner. I do not believe spirit makes mistakes, and certainly does not lie.

Could it be that Spirit knew that Mick had taken his partner's death very hard, and I was nominated to be the one to reach out to him and hopefully bring comfort?

Could it be, accepting that "U.C" was driving this experience? it was also aware, that I would only act on dream information received about Mick, not his partner?

I am wary of appearing to be egocentric, but, it seems obvious to me that I was involved, because it was decided by "U.C.", that I should be.

Finally, none of this occurred because I requested it, or willed it to happen. I appear to have been a simple functionary with no pre-knowledge or control of these things. I feel a humility and gratitude that whatever non-material power or consciousness has made use of me, and say thank you.

Post Script

I know it is unusual to add 'Post Scripts' when writing a book, because they are normally written after the event. However, what follows happened during the writing, and is totally relevant to it. On 12th June 2021, I was writing about the above events above. If you recall, I said that since that occasion, I had made a point of keeping in touch with him, because I had a strange sense that I was supposed to do so. As you may imagine, writing that, served as a reminder to contact him the next day, as I had left it a little longer than I usually did, which made me feel guilty. So, one of my last thoughts that day, was a reminder to myself to call him early the very next day.

The very next morning, 13th June 2021, I was woken up at around 9.30 am by a phone call from his wife Pam informing me that Mick had died a few weeks prior. I knew he had some health issues, but that he was responding well, and the prognosis was very hopeful. Sadly, he had contracted Coronavirus, which had led to his demise. Understandably, Mick's whole family, were so upset that they had not been able to inform everyone immediately. As you may realise, these events were taking place during the Coronavirus pandemic, and were creating additional social difficulties. We had known each other for more than sixty years, and from our first meeting, outside of my time in South Africa, and three years or so, when I first moved to Cornwall, we had been in contact with each other either personally or on the phone, on a regular basis. His death hit me very hard, more so perhaps, because I had left contact a little longer than usual, prior to his death. But, in the midst of all this, we can still be surprised at how the world decides to work.

Over a two day period, I spent some time talking to his wife and his two sons, who I have a high regard for, when suddenly, one of them reminded me that Mick's funeral took place on 12th June 2021, at which point, I realised, that at the very time of the funeral, I was writing about the portentous, but mistaken dreams about his demise many years previously, and the schoolboy humour that we shared. I do not know how this will be viewed by you dear reader, and I do not want to be fanciful, but I sense that this is possibly a bit more than synchronicity. As usual in these circumstances, I find it can be good to park the thought for a while, and see if the answer comes.

More than anything, I hope this 'Post Script' serves as my little epitaph to Mick, with whom it was a great pleasure to share my earth walk. It is my wish that my contact with his remaining family continues, and I know that I will continue to experience an enduring sadness at the vacant space he has left.

Chapter 10

We are eternal consciousness, who experience our life walk in a mutually caring partnership with our mortal human selves.

There have been occasions in my life, when intuition has made me step in and assume responsibility for things in which I would not usually have become involved. The next incident, is one such, as it represents, something of which I had no experience, or knowledge. My daughter and her family had bought a house a couple of villages away from us. Curiously enough, it was a house that my wife and I had viewed previously, but did not buy. It was formerly owned by a vicar and his wife. He had died prior to us viewing the house, and his wife subsequently lived in the house alone, which was the case, when my daughter and family purchased it. Before they moved into it, they did some fairly extensive alterations and refurbishments, in order to release its potential as a home in which to bring their children up. Because I had the skills and the time, I was happy to offer as much physical help and advice as I could. This was a joy to me, as it allowed me to pay my daughter back for all her help, when we were refurbishing our house.

The occasion of which I talk, occurred a short while after they had moved in, but we were still working in the children's bedroom. I made some comment about what a pleasing house it was becoming, when my daughter said she agreed with me, and was glad they had bought it. However, she went on to tell me that they were being disturbed regularly, by a presence in their bedroom, which was affecting their sleep. We discussed what we thought it was, and came to the conclusion, that it was probably the spirit of the deceased vicar, who had died in the house. Let me be quite clear, we are both very hands on practical folk, so, this is not something to which either of us usually gave a lot of thought, and it was actually a bit surprising to us, that we were both so ready to accept the possibility that this was in fact the cause. I could see that it was distressing my daughter quite badly, and realised that the situation would need to be dealt with, when I heard myself say to her, "You go out of the bedroom and shut the door, and I'll deal with it". I had not anticipated I would do this at all, and the phrase, "That's another fine mess you've got me into", passed fleetingly through my mind. It may have just been the automatic reaction of a father protecting his child, I do not know, but, I am more than pleased to say that, for both the living, and those in spirit, the situation was resolved.

Through all my reading and experience, although, as I've said, not formally religious in any way, I was comfortable with the principle of us being dual beings, having both physical and spiritual form, and this helped guide me in what I did. As the door closed, I sat on the bed, and began to talk to who I presumed was the deceased vicar, as if we were two people, simply having a face to face chat. I did not attempt to perform anything ritualised or religious, as I would not have known how to start.

So, in a reasonable manner, I simply told him in as kind a way I could, that I understood why he was still there, but, I needed to let him know, that it was no longer his place to be there, as my daughter and her family were now occupying the house, and were very happy to be there, but his presence was upsetting them, and I knew he would not want to do that. I went on to tell him that he had made a mistake in remaining behind, because, he had actually passed on from the physical world, and he now had a much happier, more fulfilling, and important place to be. I then said thank you for listening to me, wished him well, and told him he would be certain to find his way, just as soon as he allowed himself to go towards the light. I have checked with my daughter periodically, and in fact did so again, a short while ago, prior to writing this, and she informs me that they have not been troubled ever since, which is now a few years ago, and the room has since then, continued to have a very peaceful atmosphere. This served as a new piece of learning for me, which once again, I did not seek, but for which I am grateful to my daughter and family, and also to the now happily settled spirit of the vicar, for allowing me to help.

I have a dislike for the term ghost, when relating incidents like this, because it is a word often used to introduce titillation into low budget television shows about hauntings that try to spread fear and cheap thrills. I much prefer using the term spirit or soul, which for me aligns more acceptably with how I feel we should speak of them. In a couple of houses in which we have lived, I have been aware from time to time of the presence of spirit, but because their presence was always benevolent, even sometimes playful, we were always happy to co-exist with them. So, I have no experience of exorcisms whatsoever, and, while I suppose, it could be said that I did an exorcism, to me, that word has negative connotations, such as eradicating, or dispelling an entity with which you did not wish to engage. I would much rather remember what I did at the time, as two points of consciousness engaging caringly in communicating with each other, to achieve a mutually beneficial outcome. The term 'Win-Win', is often thought to be appropriate when a mutually beneficial agreement is made, and I feel that it fits very well in this instance.

Maybe, we should try to remember, that these spirits, are the same as us, in fact they are us. The only difference is, that we currently still inhabit our physical bodies, while they now inhabit their non- physical form, so, it behoves us to be just as caring and well-mannered as we are to everyone in our physical world. I have no intention of seeking a new career in Exorcism. But, I have learnt a lot from this, and I would now be comfortable repeating this experience, and would have no hesitation in doing exactly as I did in my daughter's house, if I felt my increased understanding would be of help.

Reflecting on this, I feel it would be wonderful, if as a society, we could now begin to take a more sophisticated and less sceptical view of life, by accepting that the things we have always intuitively and instinctively known since we began walking the earth, are very real, and play a very beneficial part in our lives. I also feel that by stubbornly clinging on to the materialist mantra, which denies that the non-material exists, also prevents us from experiencing the mystery and seeing the magic, that is nevertheless there, whether we believe in it or not. Could it be that as a species, we need to be more confident, that the experience we have gained from the time we have been on earth, allows us to place more trust in ourselves, and question the scepticism of materialist science more?

Chapter 11

**"About all we know about consciousness is that it has
something to do with head rather than the foot".**

Physicist Nick Herbert

Materialist science has a problem with consciousness because,
while grudgingly admitting that it exists, it defines it as a problem,
and finds it virtually impossible to quantify using its materialist
framework. Where for instance does it reside, what does it weigh,
what are its dimensions, and how does it allow us to feel pain,
pleasure, see colour, and feel love, joy or sorrow? These questions
and many more are a long way from being answered by materialist
scientists, who, while failing to answer such questions, still
challenge now proven non-material scientific effects, such as
learnt bio-feedback, or self-regulation for various physical, and
behavioural conditions, such as heart rate and blood pressure,
and on such conditions as OCD etc. These are the mind's (a non-
material concept) obvious control over the physical (material/
physical) function of the body. The fact that psi ability has been
proven beyond doubt, in controlled studies over many years, and

the fact that the placebo effect is now so substantially proven, that drug companies are expected to compare the efficacy of new drugs, against placebo, to ensure a minimum 5% difference between new drugs efficacy and placebo effect, is now, if not accepted universally, is expected and conformed to, in order to achieve licences for new drug treatments. Despite this, Materialist science fights hard against integrating the very obviously real and beneficial effects of all non-material phenomena, into our current paradigm. I believe this, not only hampers the expansion and reinvigoration of our wold view and the success with which we live our lives. I also believe it deters our evolution into fully realised human beings, comfortable in the knowledge, that as well as the everyday material world, we also have the privilege of access to the panoply of joyous and beneficial experiences that living in a non- material conscious world affords us.

Imagine living in a world where there was wide general acceptance of, and understanding that acceptance of the placebo effect, enhanced its power to the point where its use was preferable in appropriate cases, to the cost and toxic side effects of many if not all pharmacological drugs. Please understand! This is not a tirade against what is often called Big Pharma! I probably would not be alive today, if it was not for modern drug treatment. However, I do not accept that we continue to treat placebo effect as an aberration, when its uses could be positively reviewed, researched and integrated into treatments where appropriate. Seeking the most efficacious treatments should be at the start, middle and end of our research, not slavish, rigid adherence to any particular viewpoint.

The depth and extent of the affect that consciousness has on our lives is huge, It is far beyond my ability to quantify it, and I feel it would be presumptuous of me to try, suffice it to say, that I believe that not only are we conscious beings, enjoying all the enhanced experiences that that brings. We also have the benefit of living in a world that is conscious, in a very real sense. I believe that the world, being conscious, is aware, benevolent and watchful of our activities, and is responsive to the point of interceding at times, in order to keep us safe. We are not on the outside, looking in, I believe we are as integral to the experience, as is the greater global, probably Universal Consciousness. It is my view that our existence is not based on being separate from, I believe it is about unity, oneness and mutuality.

Not being formerly religious, I do not think of Consciousness in terms of it being a Deity, what organised religion would call God. I do not specifically have a problem with the term God, it is simply that what my senses register, appears to bear little relationship with the story the bible, particularly the Old Testament disseminates. That God, from my past reading and understanding, is a jealous, vengeful and warlike individual, who is prepared to love us providing we behave according to his laws, but is not above acts of retribution and revenge, when they are broken. While I remain unsure what to call, Universal Consciousness, I am sure that it does not sit in judgement of us, ready to rain hellfire and damnation on us in retribution for our sins. I sense no hierarchical system whatsoever, I obviously feel subordinate to that consciousness, and I am comfortable with that, but my intuition tells me that "UC", Universal Consciousness, or "U.C" which is the term I use from now on, does not view the relationship as hierarchical in any way at all. What I sense is that "UC" views the relationship as a "single status" one, with 'us' sharing equivalent importance, if not influence and power.

Writing this is a challenging exercise for me, and is taking much soul searching, because although I have unwittingly, and I hasten to add gladly had these unsought experiences, I have never set out to dissect my understanding of them in quite this much detail. So, to put it as succinctly as I can, I sense only love, complete and overwhelming benevolence. I also register interest, involvement, total care, affection, complete connection and joy. Beyond this is only a sense of limitless oneness and unity, where there is no separation. I think I have expressed the opinion somewhere that the problem with all religions is that the followers all believe their god is the true one, and they surround that with doctrine, that has seen many wars fought in its various names. This is why I have never been involved in formal religion, I have always said, God is not Christian, Muslim, Jewish, Buddhist, Hindu or anything else, He simply is. This continues to encapsulate what I believe. Universal Consciousness is not a religion it simply is. I do not believe there is a requirement for doctrine when it becomes accepted that there is only one thing necessary, and that is love. If love is not involved in anything you propose, then I believe it should not be done.

Before moving on to the next chapter, and the most life changing and transformational experience, I would like to list a number of unsought experiences that were unusual and left me wondering why.

A few years ago, when my son and I were working together, we received a call from a couple who lived in a village around twenty miles from us. Mostly our work came from domestic customers, from a wide area. Because of this, it meant that to a large degree, we had not met, or had any prior knowledge of the people, and had mostly not worked in the particular village before. For these people, there were a number of jobs to be done, and the customers invited us in to the house so we could assess the work, and led us upstairs. At this point neither of them had spoken more than a few words, when, out of the blue, I said to her, "You're a Hypnotherapist aren't you"? which indicated that I already knew the answer, and I just needed her to confirm that I was correct. Notice, I did not ask, are you a hypnotherapist? which would have required a Yes/NO answer, that would have indicated that I did not know the answer. At this point, she turned, gave me a surprised look, and said "Yes, how did you know?" to which I simply replied that I did not know how I knew, I just did. That was the end of that short, but curious experience, to which, I cannot offer anything more, except to say that, I still have no idea why or for what reason, that information was given to me, or from where it came.

I do believe that there was consciousness behind it, and everything happens for a reason, but to this day the reason remains a complete mystery.

On another occasion, we were at a social event one evening, which included a talk. It was a fairly informal gathering, and so we could interact with each other, the seating was arranged in a circle. The subject of the talk evades me now, and is not relevant, what I do remember, is that my eye kept being drawn to a lady sitting on the other side of the room. I had never seen her before, and you could say that it is not unusual, that people 'take your eye' for many reasons, and I would agree with you. However, every time I looked at her, I saw her in dark blue senior nurse's uniform, with an elasticated belt round her waist. It is possible that these uniforms are not current now, but although she was actually dressed in normal attire, this was the way she constantly appeared to me. I mentioned it to my partner, who looked, but did not see what I was seeing. So, at the end of the talk, I went over to her and introduced myself, and making apologies for doing so, I told her how I kept seeing her. She seemed pretty unfazed by this, and told me that she had been in nursing for over thirty years, and recognised the uniform I was describing. Once again, I have no explanation for why this occurred. Hopefully by now, you will have gathered that I am not an egocentric. Although I love people and really enjoy interacting with them, I have no desire to be the centre of everyone's attention. So, it is a push for me to even consider that "UC", deems me important enough to ensure that these experiences are given to me, however, I do believe that, like everything that happens, they are driven by consciousness, so, I say thank you.

As I have said many times I have not sought out unusual experiences. This has been for a number of reasons. Primarily I suppose it was because I was always too busy with the daily dynamics to have the time to do so, and my aspirations were usually more about being able to achieve practical goals such as replacing a window, painting a wall, going surfing or a walk in the country. Having said all of that, there had always been a contemplative and inquisitive side to me that made me want to discover more about the strange and unusual world that, although not looked for, was nevertheless being revealed to me. It was this that made me attend a few classes of a Psychic Development course. I am having some difficulty describing what occurred one evening, because, unusually, it placed me in a situation where, out of character for me, I was asked to stand at the front of the class, connect, and give an in depth description of the host's family house, that she had lived in as a child. What occurred was uncomfortable, because I felt connected to someone who was no longer in the physical world. My host told me that I was connected to the spirit of her father, at which point, not meaning to be unkind, I said that I felt uncomfortable and did not like him, because he had an overbearing and militaristic attitude. To this, she told me that he was a military man, but not to worry, as she did not like him in life very much either, and said please carry on, and to give as detailed a description of her home as I could. Here, it becomes even more curious, because I found myself standing in front of everyone, with a very clear picture in front of me of the outside of the building, which I described. At this point, I can hear the sceptics saying that it is fairly easy to give a loose description of the average suburban house, and most people would be fairly easily misled. I would for once, agree with the sceptics, if this had have been the case, however the house I was seeing, and I swear the host had not told me this, and there was not a photograph of it where we were attending the class, was a stone built manor house, with ivy growing up the walls, sitting on a gravelled driveway, with an arched counter-battened oak front door complete with traditional locks and hinges.

I then went through the door, and proceeded to give a full description of the entrance hall, with parquet floor, the staircase which swept round on the left, had a carpet runner up the centre, and had oak bannisters and newel posts. There were stained glass windows on the left as you ascended. I described the main living room, position and style of the fireplace, which was stone, and to the right as you entered. It had silver candlesticks at either end, and there were also photographs in silver frames on the mantle-piece. The host confirmed that my description was entirely accurate. I cannot vouch for her truthfulness in this although I did find her a credible person. What I can attest to is that the description I gave was exactly in accordance with what I was seeing in my mind's eye. I had not done anything like this before, and it left me with some very mixed feelings, because I had never had any aspirations to become involved, in connecting with spirit in this manner, which I would call Clairvoyance, and certainly not to perform what I would call 'Remote Viewing', which although interesting, it seemed as though I was involved in a fairly facile performance. From my point of view, I feel that what happened was authentic. I did feel connected to 'someone', and accept that that entity could have been the spirit of my host's father. However, I felt a genuine and unusual dislike for the entity to which I was connected, and although I still feel there was value in experiencing 'Remote Viewing', as it could be useful at some point, my overall emotion was that the whole experience was over manipulated, and done for trivial reasons.

I hold quite firm views on this, and while I accept that the ability to remote view could be very useful at some point, and that if "UC" felt it would be useful at a future date then I would retain the ability. I did not return to the course, because I felt uncomfortable with learning such practices as a taught subject. I do believe that the universe is conscious, meaningful and purposeful. I know that

"UC", Universal Consciousness exists, and from my experiences, I know and trust that it will step in and interact when necessary therefore, there is little need for us to fabricate situations in which to learn them, simply trust and things will be given when needed. I am of the opinion that it is meant to be as uncomplicated as I have experienced it to be, otherwise I believe I would have been shown something different.

The next experience is one which underscores what I have written about in the previous chapter. We had been at a friend's house about twenty miles from where we lived, for an evening of group meditation, which was a regular weekly event. We enjoyed it because as a group of usually six, we got along well, enjoyed the social aspect of it, and the sharing of our experiences afterward. The meditation was guided by one of us in turn, but I confess I would opt out of that duty whenever I could, because it meant that the one guiding could not really meditate, and I love to meditate. Half way through the evening, we would take a break, discuss anything we wanted share about the meditation, and then have a cup of tea, and a general chat. This was often followed by another period of meditation, and the evening would end around ten thirty or so, sometimes later. One evening, we fell into a conversation about parents, and the relationship we had with them, were they still alive, and so on. When I was asked, I said that I had been blessed with having my mum around until she was ninety two years old. But, that I had lost my father when I was in my early twenties, and he was only sixty four years old.

I went on to say that sadly, my father was very disconnected from myself and my siblings, and as a consequence we had never had a relationship to speak of, and I felt that there was a hole in my life where my father should have been, so he did not influence my life as he probably should have. There was a fairly wide consensus in the room, that this experience was a fairly common one, and was to an extent, a generational thing, to which I agreed. I remember saying that I did not feel anger over it, rather a sense of a lost opportunity for both my father and myself to have known each other. I also remember telling everyone, that even as a young man, prior to becoming spiritually aware, I had said on a number of occasions, that when I saw my dad again, we were going to have a conversation about the situation. None of this was angst ridden it was just conversation that could probably be anticipated, between a group of people in a similar age group.

My partner and I left later than everyone else that evening, at around midnight. It was a wet and windy night, and there were very few, if any people around as we drove out of the city to go home. The route home took us through a lovely village in a wooded valley. It is pretty much what I call a strip village, with houses on either side of the straight 'B' road. Because of the late hour and the wet, windy weather, all the house windows were closed and dark, as were our car windows, and there was no-one moving around outside on the street. I do not know what we were talking about at the time, but it was something inconsequential, when suddenly, there was an overpowering smell of pipe tobacco. It was so strong that we both remarked on it at the same moment. It was so powerful, I was trying to turn around and look in the back of the car, while asking my partner, was she sure that there was no-one in the back, smoking a pipe. We were driving at 30mph, and the smell lasted for no more the twenty seconds, and went as instantly as it came. This was followed, perhaps fifty to a hundred yards down the road by another instantaneous blast of tobacco smoke, lasting for about twenty seconds, before dissipating instantly. We were definitely surprised by this, but did not find it spooky or scary, and other than the surprise, my reaction was to state that it was my father, who smoked cigarettes and a fairly pungent brand of pipe tobacco. I felt certain that it was him responding to the conversation earlier in the evening, in the most recognisable way possible, in an attempt to let me know that I had been heard.

This is a classic case of a spiritual event occurring, when "UC" decides to act, rather than it being sought. As usual, I have passed this event through my B/S filter, so that I can be as certain as possible that you will see it as authentic and credible as my experience of it was.

1. The group we had been at was not a séance, we were not calling up spirits, or involved in any religious or bizarre practices. It was simply meditation in a group, rather than solitary meditation.
2. The weather was very wet and windy, and it was winter time, so the smoke would not have been from a bonfire.
3. All the houses were locked bolted and barred, and there was no-one on the streets, so the tobacco smoke could not have been from a villager's pipe.
4. The tobacco smell came and went in an instant on both occasions. There was no actual smoke, just the powerfully

pungent smell, real tobacco smoke does not clear instantly, it takes time, and can even be detected in a car hours later.

5. Because this event occurred after the discussion that took place earlier in the evening, I can't construe it as random I can only believe that Universal Consciousness determined that it would take place.

6. Obviously, this indicates a link between "UC" and my father's spirit, but more than this I cannot give an opinion, only to say that in the non-material world, it is accepted that everything is one, there is no separation, only unity. All I can attest to is that it took place as I have described.

7. Neither my partner or myself smoke.

Chapter 12

Nirvana is not the blowing out of the candle.
It is the extinguishing of the flame because day is come.
Indian Poet, Tagore. 1861 – 1941

I find this quotation really beautiful, and have prefaced this chapter with it because it indicates to me the transformational way of being and thinking that takes place, when one becomes spiritually aware. It speaks to me of perception being hampered, like seeing in artificial light, i.e. a candle compared to real clarity of perception, like the clarity of vision in bright daylight, i.e. because day is come. These things are of course subjective, but the way I process it, I feel it makes a beautiful preface to this chapter, which relates the most transformational, life changing, and perception altering events that have happened in my life, because, they offer conclusive certainty that consciousness continues at the end of our physical existence. These beliefs are increasingly accepted by many people, from many walks of life, many belief systems, who live their lives practicing in many disciplines. As someone who has always had a dislike for doctrine and dogma, and has never followed a prescriptive path through life, I feel humility, privilege, and immense gratitude that these experiences have been given to me. Have they changed my life? Yes! Have they made me a better person? Hopefully! but that judgement is not mine to make. Have the experiences been beneficial? Yes, in many ways. Most of all, I hope that this resonates with you Dear Reader, and that it brings all the beneficial things it has brought to me.

Studying to become a Clinical Hypnotherapist around the turn of the 21st century opened my mind in more ways than I expected. Not only to how our minds work, how we process events and experiences, but how the non- material, in the form of the spoken word, can drastically change how we construe what we are told under hypnosis, to yield beneficial changes to what are often self-damaging behaviours or beliefs. I also realised that I enjoyed having to read widely about the Hypnotherapy process, and the reading of case studies, prior to writing fairly lengthy monthly essays, as verification of my evolving knowledge. I enjoyed the learning process so much, that I found myself enthused by reading books on Neuro science, Quantum mechanics and what I call frontier science, such as Out of Body experiences (OBE's), and Near Death Experiences (NDE's).

Most of these books, I discovered were written by people very well qualified in the medical sciences, who were courageous enough to step outside of the established materialist system, and report on things for which materialist science did not have an explanation, and therefore largely denied the existence of, or could be dismissive, even disdainful. Over the years, I have learnt that the cases included in these books are well researched, well verified and are written with great sincerity and a genuine desire to propagate the power and beauty that is to be found in this non-material realm, where new perceptions and beliefs are to be found, that can enhance all our lives.

A few years ago, after being married for more than four decades, my wife was diagnosed with terminal Cancer, the prognosis was that she had about two years to live. This was devastating to us, our four children, grandchildren and wider family and friends. There are no instruction books for dealing with the devastation that such diagnoses bring, and reactions must vary widely. What we tried to do is to keep life as agreeable and enjoyable as possible. We had always enjoyed sharing our lives with family, so we continued to do this, finding extra sweetness in the simple pleasures we had always enjoyed, while trying to remain upbeat and positive.

It was during the later stages of my wife's illness, when the inevitable event was getting more imminent, that I read a book that had a huge effect on me, my wife, and events that occurred after my wife's demise. Most of the books I had read, because of their subject matter, promoted a belief that the near death experiences of which they were written, obviously supported the view that death was not the bleak end of life that most people feel very anxious about, rather, death was the beginning of a new existence in a non-material (spiritual) realm, that is very different, but probably from all indications, better and more fulfilling than our mortal life. However, the most recent book, I had read, posited the specific belief in survival of consciousness beyond life. It was the use of that sentence that drew my attention, and made me read the book enthusiastically. It indicated to me that while the writer, a person very well qualified in the medical sciences, had researched the book so thoroughly that he felt comfortable in writing about such non-material subjects that could have drawn criticism, even disdain from his peer group, wanted to do so, using the language of medical science, i.e. referring to the spirit or soul as consciousness. This book was the product of huge scientific medical knowledge and experience, and together with his undoubtable sincerity that I found his reasoning extremely compelling. Because I have a love for science, I appreciated his efforts to conform to the language of science, while expressing intangible, non-material beliefs. There were two specific items of information he expressed very clearly that appealed to me. One was that the brain does not have sufficient neurons, i.e. does not have a large enough storage capacity, to contain everything that we are, in terms of all the non-material consciousness things, such as our hopes, dreams likes, dislikes, memories, thoughts etc. the list is almost endless. I have since read this opinion expressed by Neuro- scientists elsewhere. Secondly, he expressed the opinion that our consciousness, being non-material, is never a part of our corporeal body, and therefore sits outside of our body, in what he calls, non-local space, and never being part of our physical body, does not die when our body dies, and this is why our consciousness is eternal, i.e. our spirit or soul continues.

Very simply put, which is an exercise I have to do for my own benefit. What I understand from this book, is that our consciousness, (our spirit or soul), will not fit into our brain. Being intangible, it sits in non-local space, outside of our body.

I understand non-local space, as a quantum physics term, and I am comfortable with it, but those of us with no formal allegiance to the science world, would probably feel more at home with the term Aura field, for where our consciousness (spirit or soul) resides. At one point in the book, the author explains that on reading his book, some people in circumstances that mirrored the situation my wife and I were in, had agreed between themselves, that the terminally ill partner would attempt to send a message back as proof of survival, with confirmatory results. I have no desire to write an in depth precis of the book, but suffice it to say that I found it so convincing, that I felt compelled to discuss it with my wife, so please read on Dear Reader.

You may remember from earlier in the book, that I described my wife as a very busy individual, who while not disdainful, did not spend much time on spiritual matters. But she knew that I had been researching such subjects for many years, and while not becoming involved, always said that she was happy that I had something about which I felt so enthusiastic. During the course of our marriage, and her illness, we had always been very truthful with each other, so, I took the decision to take a direct, but conversational route. I simply said to her, that we both knew that she was going to die, and that neither of us wanted that to happen, and then went on to tell her, that the book I had just finished reading, was the most credible book on the survival of consciousness beyond life that I had ever read, and I wanted to tell her about it, if she agreed. Obviously putting all her usual resistance behind her she said that she would listen. I then went onto tell her, that what I had read was to me very credible, because of the credentials of the writer, and his clear desire to promote his findings utilising the concise language of his chosen profession. I told her that I was convinced of the case he made for the survival of consciousness after physical death and that if she so wished, she could send me a message after she died, and I knew that I would receive it. She was full of questions, such as, how would I receive the message? How would I know that it was her? What if she forgot the message, and so on. This whole subject was of course, highly emotive, and I understood all of her misgivings, particularly about forgetting the message, because we had just discovered that the cancer had recently been discovered in her brain, but at that time, and until she died, she remained mentally in control of her faculties.

There are no text books that you can access to research this stuff, I had to run on my intuition, so I told her that the most important thing was that she agreed to send me a message of her own free will, and not to worry about me knowing that the message was from her, because we would agree privately, between the two of us, and not even tell anyone, either what the message was, or that we had made an arrangement for her to do so. I then told her that I really had no idea how I would get the message, but not to worry, because I was sure that it would reach me. To answer her question about her forgetting the content of the message, still flying on intuition, and in order to be as reassuring as possible, I said that she did not need to worry at all, because, once she agreed, she would not forget. The curious thing is that as I said all of this, I knew that I was speaking the truth.

My wife was never the most evidential person, and I do not recall her ever showing fear. In that she was remarkable, but there must have been moments when she was immensely frightened. So my motivation for telling her everything was partly to be able to offer her some real solace, as well as to convince her to send me a message.

I do not know why I read that particular book at that time, but I accept that "UC" was instrumental in it and as usual, I offer my appreciation, because it all worked in the most spectacular and convincing manner, as you will learn, as you read on.

A matter of weeks later, the inevitable happened, my wife died. I have no wish to dwell on this event, as I do not wish this to be mawkish or gloomy. Suffice it to say that life becomes overwhelmingly grief filled, and runs on automatic pilot for some time, while you go through a process of grieving, assimilation, and dealing with imperatives such as funerals and so on. I had been a member of a local gym for some time, and I would go there occasionally while my wife was ill, when I could safely leave her for a short while, as it kept me balanced, and altered my focus briefly. In order to put some structure into my life after she died, my routine became built around going to the gym at around eight thirty every day, because it made me get out of bed in the morning, allowed me to socialise with people, and become as fit as I could be. Other than this, my life was a process of going through the motions.

Then one evening I went to an event in Truro, possibly three months after the death of my wife. I had no presentiment that it would happen, and I was still grieving so intensely that my only expectations were to get through each day in one piece. But a meeting that evening, was the point at which I began to receive absolute and verifiable confirmation that we do live in a conscious universe, and that that what I call "UC" is aware, takes notice, and responds appropriately, always it seems, in a benevolent manner. At the end of the evening, I fell into conversation with a very special lady and another man. None of us had ever met before, and we lived in villages around twenty miles from each other. We became absorbed in our conversation to the extent that when everyone else left, as the event was held in a pub, we ordered coffee and continued chatting. I have bad knees and am awaiting knee replacements that were delayed, because I was my wife's carer, and of course her care took precedence. At one point, I said something about my knees aching, and Sarah, my new friend said that she was Reiki trained, and would be happy to send some distance healing if I wished. As a Hypnotherapist, I am very open to the power of Reiki, but also to the principle of remote, or distance healing so I accepted with a big thank you, and we made an appointment, for one week hence on Wednesday at 12.00pm. Shortly afterwards, the evening ended, we said goodnight, and we went our separate ways.

During the ensuing week, my life continued as it did at that time, with me arising fairly early, and going to the gym on a daily basis, before doing the random stuff that filled the rest of my days. On the following Saturday, I went to visit the tutor of a new course I had enrolled on. She lived in woodland on the outskirts of the town of Bodmin, I liked her energy, and looked forward to the course beginning. The following day, I decided to join a walk in woodland, which was posted on the Meetup site on the internet. It's curious how life goes, because, when I got to the rendezvous at the posted time, I realised I was in the same area I had been in the day before. I had never been to that area prior to my meeting with my new tutor, the previous day. I had a two hour walk with the rambling group despite my bad knees, and I was happy to be in such beautiful surroundings, and in new company. The following Wednesday, the day that Sarah was to give me remote Reiki, I got up at the usual time, and prepared to go to the gym, but this particular morning, when I went to the dressing table to get my hair brush, I did something different.

Suddenly, I noticed my wife's jewellery box, and thought for the first time that I would have to do something about it, and thinking that, for the first time ever, I opened it. At the very top, in the middle, was a piece of silver jewellery that I had bought for her around thirty years previously. It always seems curious to me how these things happen, but my immediate reaction, was to take it out of the box, while thinking to myself. "That doesn't need to be there, it needs to be close to me". I then put it on the dressing table, thinking that I would get my daughter, who is a silversmith, to make me a ring out of it, so my wife would then be close to me at all times. Having done this, I left for the gym returning at twelve pm. In time for my Reiki healing, and what was to be the absolutely life changing and perception altering events that I believe anyone could wish for.

Arriving home, I went into my living room, and sat quietly during the therapy period. After about ten minutes, I felt a warmth and comfort come into my knees, and a definite lessening of the pain. At the end of the session, I was so impressed that I wanted to phone Sarah to say thank you, but at that point, we had only exchanged Email addresses. So I opened my computer, called up my Emails, in order to say thank you, and to my surprise, realised that I had received a long Email from Sarah. After a greeting, she got straight to the point by telling me she had some messages for me. I was a little surprised as I had no expectations other than the therapy she had very kindly given me pro-bono. In order that it sits alone, I want to devote a separate paragraph to it as follows.

She actually began the Email in a state of surprise, saying something to the effect of, "God Mike I don't know where this has come from, but I have some messages for you". I have you meeting with a lady in a house set in woodland, last Saturday. You felt very comfortable with her, and were happy to be in her company.

She then said. This is last Sunday, and I see you walking in woodland with a group of people, I can't recognise what the trees are, but, you were happy to be mixing with others, and were enjoying being out in nature.

Next she told me something that really surprised me, she said. I can see a jewellery box, and in the box is an item of silver jewellery, and it does not need to be in there, it needs to be close to you at all times. Later she gave me such an accurate description of the jewellery box that I would have thought she was describing it while holding it in her hands.

Finally, she told me that she had a message for me, and appearing slightly unsure for the first time, she said, I think it's from your wife. She then told me that my wife wanted to tell me that she was fit, well and happy, and she knew the truth, which is 'verbatim' what my wife and I agreed would be the message she would send. So, I believe that "UC" heard the conversation between my wife and I when she agreed to send me a message. In order to placate the sceptics, I would like to discuss this event as dispassionately as possible. Firstly, I repeat, Sarah and I had never met anywhere, at any time, she had not been to my house before, and I had not been to hers. Other than mentioning that I had lost my wife in the recent past, I did not, and would not discuss the details of my loss, at such an early stage in a relationship. In my world, it would be inappropriate to discuss something as personal, in a detailed enough form, that they could extract information they could use at a later stage.

So Sarah was not privy to any information she planned to use in clairvoyance. She is a well-educated woman with good sensibilities and is entirely sincere. At that point, and at no subsequent point, has Sarah ever said that she is a Clairvoyant or spiritual Medium. In fact, I asked her about this only recently, and she said totally unassumingly, that it is because she does not believe she is, which to me, enhances her credibility even more. At the time of the Reiki session, and her remarkable reading, we had only met on one occasion, and only exchanged phone numbers, and became friends subsequently. You can verify, that what she told me, accords entirely with what I had written earlier about my actions during the week preceding our Reiki appointment. Unless of course you are in that class of sceptic, that will insist that all of it could be a fabrication, in which case, may I suggest that you cease reading immediately, and read the daily papers, where as you know, everything will be the absolute truth?

Here I feel the need to make a plea for understanding, with regard to the final item on Sarah's reading, the message from my wife. This was to the of my best recollection, the only time out of all the times that "UC" has intervened in my life, that it has happened due to my efforts to call what happened into being. I was immensely thrilled and shocked, when Sarah gave me that particular part of the message, and I feel very blessed that it occurred because it has enhanced my life and transformed my perceptions completely. Once more, a final word for the sceptics, can anyone believe that I would taint the memory of my wife of more the four decades, in order to perpetrate a deliberate untruth? Sarah's first three messages are verifiably the truth. The message from my wife alas, has to be taken on trust, and yet is a message of great power and beauty. This whole book, in particular the events I have just related, are the reason that I have written it, in the hope that it transcends your perceptions of what happens at the end of our physical existence. Below, I have included a poem that I discussed in chapter one, which is titled "What if we died", which is my adaptation of Samuel Taylor Coleridge's poem "What if you slept". It was written in an effort to encapsulate in verse, what this book endeavours to explain.

"What if we died?"

What if we died?
and what if in death?
we discovered that our soul survived
and what if we then realised?
that our physical demise was not the end
but a wonderful new beginning,
in an eternal dimension replete with love,
harmony, joy and fulfilment,
"Ah What Then"?   Mike Brookes. 2019.

Chapter 13

After over a century of assimilation of matter-less quantum technology, and our documentation of the many ways that we experience the non-material world's effects, is it now time for us to stop our resistance, and accept that we live an infinitely connected Universe?

I never had any expectations that I would experience such life enhancing and transformational events that I have. In particular, although I did arrange with my wife for her to send me a message of confirmation that consciousness does survive our physical demise, and I was confident that I would receive an answer, when it happened, it was still a major surprise. What was also a revelation, was the hard to doubt indication that "UC" had been involved in Sarah giving me the other verifiable messages, which it seems to me, was a purposeful act, in order to ensure the authenticity of what was taking place. Having been instrumental in giving me these wonderfully revelatory experiences, I believed that "UC" would not see any further need to intervene in my life for a while, but in this, I was quite mistaken, as you will discover as you read on.

I am a real lover of fresh air, sunshine and warmth, so, given the opportunity to do so, I will be in my garden stretched out on my all-weather sun lounger relaxing in the sun. The day of my next unexpected experience, my partner had taken herself to a crafting class in the village, the weather was warm and lovely, so as soon as possible, I availed myself of the sun-lounger, and relaxed. My garden faces south, so it is easy to be in full sunshine, but I never sleep in the sun, I just really relax, often, with my straw hat over my face to give me a little bit of protection from becoming too sunburnt. For me, relaxing in this way allows me to contemplate, sometimes even meditate a little. It was on this occasion, that I had an overwhelmingly powerful experience. I purposefully have an abundance of lavender in my garden, to attract bees, and it is a great luxury for me to be on my lounger, listening to the bees at work. This is what I was doing this day, when suddenly, I had what many people call an "R.S.M.E", a Religious, Spiritual, or Mystical, Experience. This may not mean an awful lot to you, and I was unfamiliar with the term, until I found a reference to it while I was researching what had happened to me after the experience. Like many of these things, for which there is no established everyday language, we have to employ inadequate man-made constructs, in our efforts to explain them. This is never entirely adequate, and is very much so in this case. As you are aware, I do not align with formalised religion, therefore, "Religious", does not clarify the experience at all, "Spiritual and Mystical" work better though. Some two years on, I am still trying to explain the wonder, the power and the overwhelming impact this event has had on me.

There is a word that I first came across many years ago, when I decided that although not formally Christian, I should at least attempt to read the Bible, on the basis that you should not dismiss anything that you do not know about. That word is "Ineffable". It is a complicated word to explain, but means, too great or extreme to describe or to express in words, the closest I can get to the meaning is, undefinable, or unimaginable. Although it is still inadequate, "ineffable" is the best word I can find to describe my RSME. Lying relaxing in the peace and warmth of a beautiful day, in a contemplative state, I became aware of a super real clarity to everything, and in that clarity, there was infinite love, understanding, benevolence, complete connectedness, and more.

Suddenly, there was almost the crackle of static electricity in the air, I say almost, which again, is inadequate, because there was definitely the crackle of static in the air, but, my best description of it is, that it was meta-physical, everything was super-real, and magnified. In the midst of all this, I felt an overwhelming sense of someone being there, it was like this presence, suddenly zoomed down from above me, in order to observe me closely. Once again this feeling was meta-physical. This was so strong, that I instantly sat upright, eyes wide open, and exclaimed out loud, even though I was all alone in my very large walled garden. "Oh my god, there's someone with me". This event was so overwhelming, that I do not know how long it lasted. It seemed that there was so much happening, and yet, it seemed that in just a few seconds the scenario collapsed back into an ordinary experience of relaxing in sunshine on a beautiful day. The sun was warm, the birds were singing, and the bees were still busy collecting pollen. Except that that was not the whole of it, because, I had a feeling that I was being told that everything was as it should be, all would be well, we were protected, loved and so on, and so on. It did not stop there it was much more complete and comprehensive than that, in fact, what happened was "Ineffable". I had over thirty years in sales and marketing, which relied on my ability to manipulate language efficiently. As I have already stated, I am also Hypnotherapist, a therapy in which there is a greater need to use language beneficially. But, alas, in describing this experience, I have failed miserably to come near to an adequate appraisal of my experience. Some two years after, during which I have had time to assimilate the experience fully, I know that I may never be able to offer an adequate description of what happened. I feel an overwhelming level of humility and privilege, that I have been given this experience, together with a deep sense of unworthiness. I have discussed this event with some of those close to me, who have asked me who I felt the presence was, and I have not been able to give them an answer. Some have offered the opinion that it may have been my deceased wife, my brother with whom I was estranged when he died, my disconnected father, etc. I did not dismiss these suggestions at all, in fact, contact with any or all of them would be wonderful. I have never sought aggrandisement or reflected glory, that has never been my style, so I feel slightly uncomfortable with what I am about to say. The truth is, I just do not know who it was, and there is no way I can know, what I do report, is that it felt like I was in the presence of everything there is, at the ultimate ground of everything. And still words are entirely inadequate, my life has been, and is still changing as a consequence. I have a very real feeling that my understanding of life is no longer static, but will continue to grow, for how long, once again, I cannot say, I simply say thank you, and continue to ask, why me? How has this experience changed me? It may be easier to list the ways in which it has not, so to answer how it has changed me is a tall order, and requires a level of introspection that I am not naturally given to, I am more interested in what value all of this may be to others. However, I will put my reticence aside in order that understanding may be passed on. Sometimes, simplicity is good, therefore, I will attempt to list all the ways, if I stray please forgive me.

1. I am now entirely convinced that we survive our physical death, and that we are eternal. This is now an undisputable truth to me.
2. I believe we live in a Conscious Universe, and that this consciousness ("UC") is intrinsically connected to us all, and intervenes, always benevolently whenever necessary.
3. It is my belief that there is a reason for most things happening. (How many times have we all said? "Oh! That was meant to happen").
4. I do not know how much of life is random, but could it be that ("UC") co-ordinates, or is the intelligence that controls a system that has been designed to function mainly on Auto-pilot, leaving the more important events for benevolent intervention, if needed, or dare I say asked for.

5. I know that ("UC") represents an entirely altruistic and observing intelligence that operates to the best benefits of us all.

6. I believe that we are intrinsically a part of ("UC"), and are as important to it, as it is to us. There is no separation, all of life and creation is one.

7. I understand that everything is as it should be, and that despite the many deliberately wrong things being done, eventually all will be well.

There are many practical daily things that have changed for me. I have not become perfect, I doubt that will ever happen in fact I do not believe I am expected to be. I have not become pious, (perish the thought), nor have I started acting righteously, (again perish the thought). Neither have I become involved in any formal religious beliefs, I am now more than convinced that established religions will never make the world a better place, probably, because they all believe that they are the one true religion, which indicates that others are thus mistaken, which causes friction, separation, disharmony, and ultimately, possible persecution and war. If this appears judgemental, I offer my sincere apologies, and give my assurance that I will never infer that any specific religious philosophy is wrong in any way, or, offer the opinion that its believers should be disparaged for what they believe. Instead, on an almost daily basis, I find myself accepting many things that most religions promote, such as love, harmony, compassion, understanding etc. While these aspirations have always been part of my philosophy, they are now at the forefront of what I am, not for any religious doctrinal reasons, but simply because they work better. There is a deep beauty in doing something, because it works on every level, equally well for everyone to the best benefit of everything. We do not need to shroud our best motivations in any doctrine. It is unnecessary to justify acting in this way in order to support formal religious beliefs, it is sufficient unto itself. We should now have the courage to act in ways that yield the best results for everyone and everything, including the environment and the wider universe, because those actions yield the results desired, and will fulfil our wish to live in a world that is rich, harmonious, and plentiful.

8. I am now fond of saying, never annoyingly I hope. "If there's no love in it, don't do it". If you really believe this, rather than paying lip service to it, it radically changes your whole mind-set, and establishes harmony, peace, understanding and love. Whereas, acting aggressively, hurtfully, spitefully, or in any way negatively, will only result in a continuation, even escalation of your own actions. (I expect many people will say that all of this is self-evident, and it is, and yet many of us continue to act in this manner).

9. I now have great difficulty behaving in any way that is devoid of compassion, even when someone's actions are incorrect and even hurtful, I do not automatically want to be incorrect or hurtful in return, because I feel that my actions are justified, (I do not believe retribution ever is justified). I now realise that seeking revenge, or retribution, will escalate and perpetuate the situation, not solve it.

Instead, I simply try to accept that we all behave incorrectly, sometimes inadvertently, sometimes not, but nevertheless, the only beneficial way to respond, is the way that yields a positive resolution and hopefully a more harmonious relationship.

10. I am entirely aware that there are many forces at large in the world that do not connect with the best intentions, and finer sensibilities when making decisions that are hugely beneficial to themselves, while often also adversely affecting others. These decisions are made out of fear, greed, insensitivity and weakness. These systems and organisations have always been there. This way of running our systems causes untold harm, and prevents our world from evolving into the peaceful, safe and harmonious world that would benefit everyone. However, nothing will be gained from emulating, or castigating such people or systems, they are intrinsically mistaken in what they do. Nothing will change until they see that they need to change, and begin to believe in behaving differently. What we can do, is keep our hearts peaceful, walk a better path, not for righteousness or religious reasons, but simply because there is beauty and amazing power in doing what is intrinsically right, and is to the benefit of everything. I have said earlier, that I do not advocate being evangelical, one of the reasons, is that it infers that you are incorrect and I am right. Apart from being challenging and annoying, this also leads to resistance, which is the polar opposite of the effect that is sought. We are only ever responsible for our own actions,

and within the bounds of the law, we have to allow others to be responsible for theirs. So, a final word, and I am sure this has been voiced many times before in a variety of ways, "If you want the world to change, first, change yourself, and remain optimistic that the rest of the world will change when they see a good idea working".

Chapter 14

We interpret non-material/ intangible/spiritual phenomena using our native language, which often falls short of having a wide enough vocabulary, or an adequate frame of reference to do this subject the justice it deserves.

As we approach the end of this short, but I hope useful, transformational and uplifting book, I can almost hear you enquiring, "What else has happened, what more do we need to know?" The answer to that is that I do not yet know myself, what will happen next. The reason for this is very simple, the extraordinary life changing experiences I have had, were never of my making, it was not part of a devised plan, so that I could write a book that would hopefully reach, and be of benefit to you and many others dear reader. None of it is a product of my delusional mind, neither did any of it happen because I willed it to. I now realise and accept that "UC", has been in control of all the events that I have truthfully reported. The other simple truth is, that although, I felt compelled to write my story as it stands currently, my intuition tells me, that having come this far, "UC" has not yet finished, there will be more revelations, more interventions, and more twists and turns, I believe there will be a plan and a reason for whatever occurs. I also trust that whatever happens will yield a benevolent outcome. Because I can see that every time "UC" has intervened throughout my life, that the results have been for my safety and my ultimate benefit, I trust that whatever happens in future will be for the same reasons, and I offer my genuine gratitude.

Since my agreement with my terminally ill wife that she would survive her mortal end, and send me a message of proof, through my wonderful friend Sarah, and my R.S.M.E. in my garden. I have been experiencing many changes. I am still a very practical down to earth person. I recently was blessed with a granddaughter, my third, and have, using my carpentry skills, begun making her a stool, which I have done for all my other grandchildren. I have also made presents for birthdays etc. as well as spending time making my large garden pretty for the summer, and so on. So I am Mr. Earthbound man, and loving it. At the same time I am aware that I am evolving spiritually, I am more open with people, more willing to connect. My enjoyment and regard for the natural environment is vastly enhanced. I now have an even stronger understanding that everything is infinitely connected. I have a very single status philosophy. I now have no time for hierarchies. I believe we should not put ourselves above others, or that anyone should be put above us. In order that we can transform our world into what it should be, I believe there is an urgent need to realise that we are all one, and any action taken to the detriment of anyone, is to the detriment of us all. I value my mortal life very much, and remain extremely inquisitive and enthusiastic, but there are things that are changing in my life, things that make me wonder what for? And, again why me? and, of course, "What If". So, I am aware that things will become apparent at the right time. Life can become very easy when you realise that you were never in control in the first place, so practice humility, find peace and joy, say thank you, and be aware of the magic happening around you.

One final word, which I feel the need to include, is to repeat the reason for writing this book. At no level have I been seeking approval for what I have written, the story is an entirely a personal one, I hope I have told it as truthfully and sincerely as possible.

It was not written to massage my fragile ego, or to make gain, which includes your approval. I simply hope that the information you have read, will help you accept that our human existence and the universe in which it takes place, are more special, more connected, and more magical than we commonly perceive them to be, and it is my sincere wish that you find the transformational belief and understanding that we are all eternal, that our consciousness survives our physical demise, and that you live the life of joy that you seek and deserve. Finally, it is my profoundest wish that we all learn that we should only act with love, simply because it is the one thing that will yield what we all need, nothing else is quite so certain.

Afterword

I feel very privileged to have been given the experiences that have led to the writing of this book. I wrote earlier, that I am aware that as humans, probably our greatest fear is the fear of our ultimate demise. We live our physical lives with the persistent awareness of our mortality. I believe that this has a limiting effect on our happiness, as so many of us view death as the nothingness that awaits us all. My experiences lead me to believe that our consciousness, what I am happy to call our souls, survive our physical death, and that we are actually eternal beings. I also believe that as souls, we can and do enjoy beneficial two-way communication between spirit and our physical selves. There are many beliefs and theories about what happens to us ultimately. I feel convinced that we resurrect, but knowledge of this is not currently mine, I am convinced though, that "UC" does things for a purpose, and we are not given our physical lives, and the gaining of all that knowledge and experience, for it to have no value simply because our bodies have worn out. I believe that we have intrinsic value and importance to "UC" and that the purpose will ultimately be made apparent.

The reason for writing this book therefore was to share my experiences with you, in order to offer certainty that we are eternal, and that we are an intrinsic part of a very well established and valued plan, and that we should live our lives with increased joy and positivity, and discard the anxiety and fear we unnecessarily allow to mar, what it is to be human. If any of what I have written offers peace, love, comfort, increased joy and understanding, then I will be entirely satisfied with my efforts.

The loss of my wife in 2017, caused many changes in family relationships, obviously, this created the desire to write this book. As a grandfather of many grandchildren, I have been aware that the loss of their Granny, caused the younger ones to become aware of their own eventual mortality for the first time. It also caused me to recognise that I felt an unspoken anger towards me, because, as the remaining Grandparent, it was somehow, my fault. These things are subtle, but there was a change in their relationship with me. Obviously, I was and have always been concerned about my grandchildren's wellbeing, so I asked my daughter's permission to explain to them about this book, my reasons for writing it, and how I hoped it would help everyone in this situation. Being the sensitive, intelligent and perceptive children they are, they understood what they were told, and it has transformed their understanding, and hopefully allowed closure and acceptance to occur. Their relationship with me is now everything I ever hoped it could be, because they understand that the end of life is not an end, but a continuation in a non-physical, rewarding and eternal state as our ultimate eternal selves.

The End

Lightning Source UK Ltd.
Milton Keynes UK
UKHW040900101222
413706UK00001B/127